The Harvest Prayer of Jesus

Why American Christians are Missing
Today's Global Renewal

Edward N. Gross

Foreword by Dr. Aila Tasse

&

Parson's Porch Books

www.parsonsporchbooks.com

The Harvest Prayer of Jesus

ISBN: Softcover 978-1-951472-49-8

Copyright © 2020 by Edward N. Gross

All Scripture quotations, unless otherwise indicated, are taken from the English Standard Version Bible copyright 2001 by Crossway, a publishing ministry of God News Publishers.

The Harvest Prayer of Jesus

Contents

Support for *The Harvest Prayer of Jesus* 5

Dedication 13

Foreword 17

Chapter One 21

The Harvest Prayer

Chapter Two 25

Do YOU Pray the Harvest Prayer? 25

Chapter Three

Falling in Love with Prayer 28

Chapter Four 31

Accepting the Relevance of the Harvest Prayer TODAY

Chapter Five 37

What Follows The Harvest Prayer?

Chapter Six 45

When the Train Hops the Tracks

Chapter Seven 53

Why NO DMMs in the USA?

Appendix One 61

Jesus' Seven Invitations to Pray (John 14-16)

Appendix Two 63

Who were the 72?

Appendix Three 66

    Receptivity: The Mark of a Person of Peace

Appendix Four 70

    The Rest of the Luke 10 Story

Appendix Five 74

    Helpful Quotes on Prayer

Appendix Six 96

    Praying through the Kingdom Parables

Endnotes 98

Support for *The Harvest Prayer* of Jesus

From the USA

In the 21st century church, **Jesus' first command to his 12 disciples regarding how to launch other disciples has probably been his most ignored command of all.** *Yet it was the most obvious element: "Pray the Lord of the harvest to send out laborers into his harvest."*

In a compact and insightful new book, The Harvest Prayer of Jesus, Edward Gross has provided Christ Followers a useful resource that will help all of us experience prayer that guides and empowers fruitfulness at each level of the disciple making process.

Jerry Trousdale
Missionary, Pastor, Author
Co-Founder of Final Command,
Director of International Ministries: New Generations

Dr. Gross has struck at the heart of why the Church in North America is in decline. Harvest Prayer is something that most of us have never thought about, much less prayed. The essence of his message to us, as disciples of Christ, is found in the words, "When God, who is love (1 John 4:8,16,) gives you the gift of love for Himself and others, then true prayer is born in your heart." Ed is challenging us to return to our first love, which begins and ends each day in intimate prayer with God. This book challenges us to re-examine our prayer lives to the extent of making it the most important part of our lives each and every day. If you follow the steps laid out in the "Harvest Prayer of Jesus," you will not only rediscover your first love for God, but for your fellow man as well. Your prayer will become, "that none should perish, not even one!"

Richard Williams, President
Compassion for Life

Ed Gross has hit the key of seeing the Great Commission of Jesus fulfilled all over the world, which is **prayer.** *He has also shown how prayer launches into the action of reaching others with God's word. For me, the most amazing part of this book is Ed's stories of the interaction between his obedient prayer and the action of God in bringing people to him to meet Jesus. Making disciples is an active partnership between Jesus and those who will obey Him both in prayer and action.*

James A Lilly
Author of *Great Commission Disciple Making,* and *Family Disciple Making*

You can always count on Ed Gross to leave no stone unturned. Despite whether you agree with him or not, this book is worth owning! It is a time-saving resource for diving into the depths of prayer in the Bible. You could spend hours doing what Ed has already done for you on a topic, prayer, which sits at the pinnacle of our spiritual journey.

Roy Moran
Author of *Spent Matches: igniting a signal fire for the spiritually dissatisfied*

Ed Gross is a voice that pastors and Christian leaders in North America should pay close attention to today. With most churches in spiritual, missional and numerical decline, Ed brings an astonishing and hopeful report of disciples making disciples in numerous corners of the world using a simple approach to the study of Scriptures combined with an earnest seeking of the Spirit of God in prayer. Ed blends rich biblical insights from years of careful study with keen insights and learning from the global church.

Take note. The Harvest Prayer of Jesus is not a program but a warm and enthusiastic call to prayer with an open heart and mind. I have no doubt that the Lord Jesus can and will renew His people through discipleship and making of disciples.

Rev. Stuart H. Spencer
Pastor/Head of Staff- First Presbyterian Church
Moorestown, NJ

The call of The Harvest Prayer of Jesus is clear and direct for anyone who calls himself a Christ follower. Men need to hear this in groups and be held accountable to this ancient but regretfully now softened command of Jesus to "Go and make disciples." The eternal destiny of so many is in the balance.

Gene McGee
On the Street Church, Men's Ministry Pastor
Philadelphia, PA

Brother Ed has simplified all of his other books into this one. Most of us involved in ministry will say regularly, that we want our ministry to grow, we want our church to grow, we want, we want, we want...but we want it to happen in our way. He simply explains that most of us are not doing it the LORD's way. If you want to do it the Biblical way, read The Harvest Prayer of Jesus and follow the instructions he lays out for us. Then we'll see your ministries bearing fruit and yielding, one hundredfold, sixtyfold, or, in another case, thirtyfold.

Rick Vincent
Chaplain, Preeminence of Christ Prison Ministries
Montverde, FL

Ed Gross offers us a powerful treasure and practical insight in The Harvest Prayer of Jesus. Read this and learn to pray this way and watch God bring the results!

Matthew Pieters
Pastor, BridgePoint Church
Valparaiso, IN

A biblically solid, Spirit led book for our historical moment. I was refreshed and further drawn into a simple, powerful obedience and increasing closeness with Jesus in total dependence on the Spirit.

John Portis
MAR Westminster Theological Seminary

Dr. Ed Gross continues to use his experiences and Spirit-led insights to guide us in the ways of Biblical discipleship with "The Harvest Prayer of Jesus." As he points out, Jesus' exhortation to His disciples to pray to the Lord of the harvest is no less significant than teaching them the Lord's Prayer or His instructions on finding a house of peace, as He later sends them out.

.

Ed captures the absolute necessity of praying "The Harvest Prayer of Jesus" - providing well-documented examples of how following His specific teachings are working TODAY around the world. And, how neglecting them has negatively impacted the fruitfulness of western culture discipleship. Ed also reinforces the need for repentance, obedience, and love, while focusing on fervent prayer to the Lord of the harvest, as all being foundational for fruitful discipleship. Read The Harvest Prayer of Jesus.

Bruce W. Cobb
Retired Master Chief Petty Officer, U. S. Navy
Former Missionary - International Mission Board

In an hour when global attention is focused on survival against a virus, Ed Gross offers hopeful biblical motivation for intentional disciple-making after the pattern of Jesus the Messiah, who calls us to follow him.

Carl T Martin, DMin.
Clearwater, FL

From Africa

No other modern day writer has influenced me more than Ed Gross. In every book he writes it is as if I am underlining and highlighting every sentence because of its importance and relevance and it is no different with this one!

My prayer is that this book will get into the hands of many Christians so that they can be moved to start praying for the harvest as they go and make disciples of all nations! This book is very important!!

Gideon Van der Merwe
Pastor - Reformed Church Pretoria-Annlin
South Africa

As Pastor Gross points out in this inspiring book, we are truly living in times of an unprecedented expansion of the gospel, and prayer is what is fueling the fire! While rightly focusing on the Lord's Prayer, Christians have glossed over Jesus' command that we pray His pivotal "Harvest Prayer." I would like to exhort Christians all over the world to start praying this prayer - with passion! Two thousand years after Jesus' resurrection and ascension, His statement that "the harvest is great, but the workers are few" still holds true. What we most need are dedicated and focused disciple-making workers to keep up with God's momentum. I wholeheartedly endorse and recommend this book to any Christian!

Hendrik Vermont, M.Th.
Ministry Director: Didasko Academy
(www.dasko.org)

The Lord of the harvest has sent Dr Ed Gross and the disciples in Zambia into the ripened fields, outside the four walls of the Church, making disciples where the church has neglected to do so. Through simple obedience, God has brought thousands of "Persons of Peace" of different age groups on our path and we have had the rare privilege to disciple them.

We have witnessed a great revival in Zambian sports, especially in soccer, leading to the birth of "Bola na Lesa" (football with God) in 2016 with the Zambia Under Twenty (U20) boys team. These disciples in soccer-shoes were sent on a mission by God and were crowned Southern African champions (2016) and African Champions on March 12, 2017! On that day, the vivid battle of light and darkness was witnessed by over a billion Africans and others globally, when the Senegalese junior team performed witchcraft live for all to see.

God has produced such lasting fruit, evidence-based disciple making, that implements the 2 Tim 2:2 formula and the model"Watch me do it; Let's do it together; Do it while I watch you with guidance and Go do it yourselves." I have known Prof Edward N. Gross for the past 14yrs and I have witnessed his personal transformation and application of what he teaches.

Elemon Sakala, Jr.
Chaplain
Zambia National Soccer Teams.
President, Victorious LIFE
Zambia

.

Dedication

I dedicate this little book to the thousands of great, brave disciples of Jesus throughout the world, who are obediently making disciples, on the foundation of faithful and earnest prayer, and, thereby, fulfilling the Great Commission of our Lord and Savior Jesus Christ

"But many who are first will be last, and the last first" (Matthew 19:30)

Foreword

I am delighted to write the foreword for the book, The Harvest Prayer of Jesus, by Edward N. Gross. We need to understand the subject of prayer if we desire a movement of God. Prayer is the key to all the Kingdom movements around the world. Of all the Kingdom movements that I know, none of them was started before leaders started praying. So, if we want to see a Kingdom movement happen, we have to be on our knees earnestly seeking God until we see His heart's desire fulfilled in the launching of sustainable, disciple-making movements (DMMs).

So many books have been written about prayer, and conferences have been called for prayer. While these are all good, many, sadly, have been turned into programs. Prayer is not a religious program; it's a lifestyle of a believer. We spiritually breathe and engage God through our prayers. What is happening to and through others, will not happen until we earnestly pray and commit ourselves to the prayer that gives birth to a movement.

The lifestyle of prayer for the thousands of us who are disciples through DMMs in East Africa is simply this: *The normal disciple spends on average three hours a day in prayer.* We spend more time praying than eating because of the vital nature of prayer. If we want to grow our bodies, we must eat. If we want to grow spiritually or to advance a movement, we must pray. And this is earnest prayer, not just like praying before eating a meal.

In fact, we distinguish three types of prayer both for us as disciples and as leaders of Disciple Making Movements: Firstly, is what we call "**Scheduled Prayer**." These are our regular times of daily prayer. Peter and John went up to the temple at "the hour of prayer" (Acts 3). This aspect of our prayer life is our fixed daily pattern which involves worship, praise, thanksgiving and some petitions. Secondly, we practice "**Concentrated Prayer**." During this time, we devote ourselves to growing our own spiritual lives, growing deeper in Christ. We also focus on special requests, burdens, emergencies that currently need our attention and God's special help. Thirdly, we are devoted to "**Continuous Prayer**," or the kind commanded by Paul in 1 Thess. 5:17, "Pray without ceasing!" This is the prayer we have at all times, whatever we may be doing. It might focus on our business, family, neighbors or whatever. We cannot do anything without making prayer the most important aspect of that activity. We live this way because that is how the New Testament era disciples of Jesus were expected to live. And that is why we also fast regularly, because they did. I fast on Wednesdays from morning to evening. During this special time many spiritual breakthroughs come in my own life and in the lives of others.

I hope this helps those of you in America and elsewhere to understand our devotion to prayer. The Church in Acts was a praying church. So must we be. The leaders of that Church were prayer warriors. I would not consider ordaining a person in ministry who was not devoted to a lifestyle of prayer. How can one lead others when the crucial element of prayer is missing? And this kind of real devotion must be to be taught and modeled by both a leader and any growing disciple. Let's be clear, our devotion to prayer is all by God's grace and by the power of the Holy Spirit; but, it demands our commitment as well. Most great things don't just happen on their own. And prayer is one of those things.

We cannot learn to pray by just reading books written on prayers or listening to someone speaking about prayer. We learn how to powerfully pray by (1) praying, (2) engaging in a prayer movement and (3) encouraging others to pray.

Edward has introduced us, in The Harvest Prayer of Jesus, to that kind of prayer life where prayer becomes a lifestyle producing disciples and disciple-makers. I'm blessed to have read through all that he has written on prayer.

Having led a growing, multiplying network of disciple-making movements around East Africa for the last 15 years, I have witnessed how God has used ordinary people to pray and receive answers which have led to the launching of movements, most of which have grown beyond 10 generations of disciples and churches. The same can happen anywhere in the world!

Prayer is something that we can all learn from the life of our Lord Jesus Christ. He prayed before he started his ministry, he prayed while doing his ministries, he prayed in the garden of Gethsemane, he prayed while dying on the Cross, and he is praying for us in heaven right now. Jesus prayed in all situations, and at all times! As his followers, so should we.

The prayer movement that was started by Jesus was continued by the Early Church as we read in the books of Acts. The early Church was born in a prayer meeting in the upper room in Acts 1. The Jerusalem Church prayed and saw a true Kingdom movement birthed. From the beginning, all those who founded and led Kingdom movements have been men and women of prayer. You will not be an exception to that pattern.

For the years that I have been involved in disciple-making movements, God has taught me that, while it's only God who can start a movement, he will involve and use those of us who are willing to pray and work with him to see movements multiply. Our place is (1) to engage God in prayer, asking "the Lord of the harvest" (2) to show us the person of peace, and (3) how to engage the community, (4) leading to developing godly leaders for a movement. This book, by brother Edward, will help you learn how to be that person who grows in developing a lifestyle of prayer and, thereby, helps to launch a Kingdom movement for the glory of our Lord Jesus Christ.

Dr. Aila Tasse
Lifeway Mission International

Chapter One
The Harvest Prayer

Is it possible that American Christians have ignored the strategy that Jesus and the first disciples used when they "turned the world upside down" (Acts 17:6)? The amazing answer is, "Yes!" That is why mission agencies, missionaries and church planters around the world by the thousands are now changing outreach and church growth strategies to the mission strategy of Jesus that has been "hidden in plain sight."[1] Let's look at what we missed for so long so that we may follow Jesus more obediently.

The Lord's Prayer has rightly been mastered and prayed by millions, since the First Century with incredible blessing. But there was another prayer which Jesus gave to His disciples to pray. And they would have mastered and prayed it word-for-word, because that is what disciples did.[2] I call this prayer, "The Harvest Prayer."

Like the Lord's Prayer, the Harvest Prayer is found twice in the Gospels. Here is the Harvest Prayer in its two different contexts:

And Jesus went throughout all the cities and villages. Teaching in their synagogues and proclaiming the gospel of the kingdom and healing every disease and every affliction. When he saw the crowds, he had compassion for them, because they were harassed and helpless, like sheep without a shepherd. Then he said to his disciples, **'The harvest is plentiful, but the laborers are few. Therefore pray earnestly to the Lord of the harvest to send out laborers into his harvest.'** And he called to him his twelve disciples and … sent (them) out, instructing them, "Go nowhere among the Gentiles and enter no town of the Samaritans, but go rather to the lost sheep of the house of Israel. And proclaim as you go, saying, 'The kingdom of heaven is at hand.'"(Matthew 9:35-10:7)

- - - - - - - -

After this the Lord appointed seventy-two others and sent them on ahead of him, two by two, into every town and place where he himself was about to go. And he said to them, '**The harvest is plentiful, but the laborers are few. Therefore pray earnestly to the Lord of the harvest to send out laborers into his harvest.**' Go your way; behold, I am sending you out as lambs in the midst of wolves…Whatever house you enter, first say, 'Peace be to this house!' And if a son of peace is there, your peace will rest upon him. But if not, it will return to you. (Luke 10:1-6)

As a missiologist, I have taught courses on the History of Missions. These courses often included scanning hundreds of strategies to "reach the world with the Gospel" throughout the history of Christianity. Not once did I see a plan that was based on carefully and prayerfully following the example of Jesus in sending out His Twelve and the 72, as recorded in the Gospels.

A Fatal Omission

What is happening TODAY throughout the world by simple disciples who are praying the Harvest Prayer and following the strategy that Jesus commanded, is absolutely amazing. Indeed, as one missionary author put it, the results are "***unprecedented.***" In his truly watershed book, *Miraculous Movements*[3], Jerry Trousdale wrote,

"…God is creating a remarkable and unprecedented momentum of ministry in some of the least expected places in the Islamic world…. In our own ministry context, 'unprecedented' is used to describe the following:

-Multiple cases of entire mosques coming to faith.

-Thousands of ordinary men and women being used by God to achieve seemingly impossible outcomes.

-Tens of thousands of Muslim background Christians becoming dedicated intercessors who fast and pray for the gospel to penetrate the next community.

-Muslim people groups that never had even one church among them now have more than fifty churches planted, and in some cases more than 100 churches—within two years of engagement.

-Former sheikhs, imams, and militant Islamists making up 20% or more of the new Christian leaders in Muslim regions."[4]

I have met and been trained by Jerry and some of these amazing disciples from Africa. They have rediscovered and restarted praying The Harvest Prayer. Then they have followed the strategy of Jesus that flows from The Harvest Prayer.

The fruitfulness in Africa has been so great, that leading disciplers there have recently recommended that we from the USA spend more time praying and working for renewals of biblical discipleship throughout America's Evangelical churches and less time in Africa! Why would they suggest this?

Simply because they believe that they can disciple Africa themselves. Africans are so fruitfully going into the harvest of Africa and making disciples there, that we should focus more on our own "Jerusalem." They are being far more successful in fulfilling the Great Commission in Africa than American Christians are here in the States.

Missionaries and disciples throughout Africa and beyond have made a discovery that we desperately need here in the USA. That is why I am writing this book and concentrating my life now mainly on helping Christians in the USA become disciples who make disciples.[5] I pray that this small book will be used by the Holy Spirit to open your eyes and move your hearts to forsake our fatal omission—PRAYER! And specifically, praying The Harvest Prayer. When disciples pray this prayer in faith, they are obeying the command of Jesus. So, we can call The Harvest Prayer, obedient prayer. Will YOU obey and *"keep in step with the Spirit"* as He graciously renews Christianity and calls new disciples to follow Jesus from all over the world?

Chapter Two
Do YOU Pray the Harvest Prayer?

What would you do, if you were a God of love, and wanted to reach the world through a family of disciples? Would you let them learn only by trial and error? Or would you clearly tell them how best to accomplish that goal? Jesus not only told them how to make disciples, He showed them how to do it. Teaching them to pray The Harvest Prayer was an indispensable element of His strategy for global renewal. The training became complete when He let them experience the victorious and fruitful situations that flowed from praying The Harvest Prayer.

As noted in the first chapter, Jesus repeated these words to both the Twelve and to the 72 as He sent them out on their training missions. Yes, Jesus sent His disciples out so that they could practice and master what it means to "Go and make disciples." You see, Jesus' discipleship training included four basic steps:

1. Watch me do it

2. We will do it together

3. I will watch and guide you doing it

4. You are ready—go do it yourselves[6]

The Perfect Disciple

Jesus embodied true discipleship. Everything He did and said was as a disciple of His Father. So, He affirmed, "Truly, truly I say to you, the Son can do nothing of his own accord, but only what he sees the Father doing. For whatever the Father does, that the Son does likewise" (John 5:19). "The one who rejects me and does not receive my words has a judge; the word that I have spoken will judge him on the last day. For I have not spoken on my own authority, but the Father who sent me has himself given me a commandment—what to say and what to speak. And I know that his commandment is eternal life. What I say, therefore, I say as the Father told me" (John 12:48-50).

How did that work in the life of Jesus? What were its dynamics? Well, the Father did not constantly appear to Jesus and physically speak to Him, telling Him what to say and where to go. As a man, Jesus was His perfect disciple. He followed the Father by faith through the power of the Holy Spirit. And that is what Jesus expects of us, His disciples. We are to follow Jesus now by faith as He followed the Father by faith when He walked this earth as the Spirit-filled Son of Man.

No Prayer, No Discipleship

So, just as prayer was central to Him, so it must be to us. Prayer is the breath of faith. Without breathing we die. Without prayer, faith dies. Jesus lived a life of prayer in the presence of His disciples and taught them to do the same.[7] When Paul commanded the Thessalonians, "Pray without ceasing," he was simply reiterating the baseline of a disciple's life. We cannot follow an invisible Master in any other way. We must constantly communicate with Him and be guided by Him. And that is not the way most of us were taught, after becoming a Christian and shown how to live "the normal Christian life." We have not been trained and shown what it means to "walk by faith, not by sight" (2 Cor. 5:7).

Twice, at least, Jesus taught His disciples to pray The Harvest Prayer: *"Lord of the harvest, send out laborers into your harvest."* Most of us do NOT pray that prayer as a regular feature of our life, if at all. We should ask Father to forgive us for not obeying Jesus in praying The Harvest Prayer at the beginning of each day and as the cornerstone of all our outreach strategies. Did you know that before the Apostles started their day, they were taught to pray The Lord's Prayer? That is proven by the fourth petition in the prayer: "Give us **this day** our daily bread" (Matt 6:11). They were taught to pray the Lord's Prayer before they ate their breakfast. And before they went out into the day, they were led to look compassionately on the lost and to pray another prayer. The Harvest Prayer. So, before we go out, we should pray the very same prayer.

Am I saying that what Jesus has promised will happen if we begin to obey Him by praying The Harvest Prayer and then proceeding as the early disciples did? That is exactly what the rest of this book will show you. But just before I show you that, you must be convinced that prayer, itself, is priceless. If you do not cherish prayer, you will not experience the special blessing of The Harvest Prayer. The amazing promises of God, the Lord of the Harvest, are being fulfilled by thousands of simple disciples whose lives are lived in the daily expectation of The Harvest Prayer! May a new season of fruitfulness open to you as you join us in devoting your life to prayer.

Chapter Three
Falling in Love with Prayer

Love is the greatest power in the world. Paul was right when he wrote, "Love never fails" (1 Cor. 13:8-NKJV). One reason that love doesn't fail is because it never gives up. The most incredible accomplishments on earth have been achieved by those who were driven by love. Every person who has fallen in love, knows how far he or she will go in pursuit of that love. In the protection of that love. But the love of God, when it replaces our capacity to love, is utterly superior. It attempts and accomplishes even greater things.

When God, who is love (1 John 4:8,16), gives you the gift of love for Himself and others, then true prayer is born in your heart. This has been the testimony of all who have been joyfully devoted to prayer. And it is my experience.

A Divine Realignment

My life was changed in the midst of my ministry. Having been a top student, successful church planter, pastor, professor and missionary, I returned back to the States, at 48 years old, only to learn that I was not filled with the love of God. I became aware of that when God used the prayers of one of my seminary students, and the preaching of our church's youth director. By God's grace, I repented and became a different man.[8]

The realization that my life and ministry were not driven by love was not that hard for me to accept. The hard step was the repentance. I had to let it sink in that I had refused to make FIRST that which mattered most to God.

Towards the end of His life, Jesus was tested by a lawyer who asked him, "Teacher, which is the great commandment of the Law?" Disregarding the motives of the man, Jesus gave what was, perhaps, the most important words ever spoken:

"And he said to him, 'You shall love the Lord your God with all your heart and with all your soul and with all your mind. This is the first and great commandment. And a second is like it: You shall love your neighbor as yourself. On these two commandments depend all of the Law and the Prophets'" (Matt 22:36-40).

My soul was undone when I realized that what matters most to God, my Creator and Redeemer, was not the priority of my life and ministry. The hard work came in giving up what had taken love's place. You see, in order to truly repent, we must remove (or seek the help of God to remove) the obstacles from our life. Both inward and outward idols must go. For me, there was no affair with another woman. Or embezzlement of church funds. But there were plenty of other sins that had to be faced, confessed and nailed to the cross.

I had to deal with the "man wounds" of my youth in relationship with mom. These had transitioned over and affected my relationship with Debby. They needed to be discovered, removed and replaced.[9] I had at times become a spiritual bully both in my speaking to Debby and from the pulpit. Since my preaching was "a public sin," I repented publically before the church. Since my sins against Debby were private, (and never physical), I repented of them before her and the kids. I could be verbally and emotionally abusive. The Spirit of God rescued me by filling me with His love. My story and new message of love have been shared in another little book, the message of which is now the foundation of my life and ministry and might be of great benefit to you.[10]

Please hear me correctly. I can only love to pray when I am filled with the Spirit of God and with his first fruit, love. Prayer is simply communicating our hearts to God. You cannot help but communicate with the one whom you love. When you are filled with the love of God, prayer will be the natural result. So, that has become my constant pursuit: the filling and flowing through me of God's love and Spirit. It should be your longing also.

Jesus dearly wants us all to fall in love with prayer. This can be seen clearly from the seven times in one setting, the Upper Room, that He uniquely and powerfully tried to focus the Apostles' attention on their necessity of living a life of prayer. At the same time, and in His amazing end-of-life prayer (chap. 17), He uses the word "love" some 31 times! The love of God (agape) and prayer are uniquely and inextricably united. The one does not exist without the other. You will not be able to regularly pray The Harvest Prayer or live a life of prayer unless you seek and are filled with the love of God. (See Appendix One – Jesus' Seven Invitations to Pray).

Chapter Four
Accepting the Relevance of the Harvest Prayer TODAY

Some will probably argue that we are not the original Apostles, so The Harvest Prayer does not apply to us. Perhaps that is why the great missionary doctor Luke gives us the second occurrence of Jesus commanding it to be prayed. He did not give it only to the Apostles. He shared this treasure "with seventy-two others" (Luke 10:1).[11] We do not know any of them by name. We just know that they were other than the Twelve. (See Appendix Two – Who were the 72?)

I think that it will help you to take a moment to consider some of the features of the sending-out that occurred in Luke 10, when Jesus sent out the 72. So, I will give you some very simple, practical notes on it, and then provide some of the amazing stories of what is happening today as people follow this same daily mission strategy.

Luke 10:1 "After this the Lord appointed 72 others and sent them on ahead of him, two by two, into every town and place where he himself was about to go."

- Luke sees no reason why he should identify these people, who were beyond the number of the inner apostolic group. I see this as giving the impression that going out like this would be a regular feature of discipleship or being a disciple.[12]
- Like the Twelve, He sent them out 2 by 2, or in pairs. The Bible mentions the importance of small groups of 2 or 3 in several places. There is greater safety in twos.

There is heightened perception, wisdom, prayer and fellowship when partnering with another. But, most importantly, Jesus promised, *"For where two or three are gathered in my name, there am I among them" (Matt 18:20).*

- The going of the 72 was connected with the specific areas in which Jesus was to minister, Himself.

Luke 10:2a - "And he said to them, 'The harvest is plentiful, but the laborers are few. Therefore pray earnestly to the Lord of the harvest to send out laborers into his harvest."

- Jesus stated that his disciples had a huge job ahead of them, that there were many people ready to be harvested or reaped for His Kingdom. The word "indeed" or "truly" is actually in the Greek text before the word plentiful. The harvest is indeed plentiful! This implies that; however things might appear or whatever the disciples might have thought about their own ability, there were truly many to be harvested.

- Given this optimistic view of the harvest, Jesus said that a problem existed—there were not enough skilled workers to do the reaping. "The harvest is plentiful, BUT THE LABORERS ARE FEW." There was a manpower problem. He, obviously, did not want to give them an impossible task. So, He designed a way to circumvent the lack of workers. He gave them a strategy by which the great task could be accomplished by a relatively small work force! And His way of solving the problem began with simply praying The Harvest Prayer.

Luke 10:2b- "Therefore pray earnestly to the Lord of the harvest to send out laborers into his harvest."

- *"Therefore…"* Because the spiritual work is so great and ready, and those who know what to do and where to go are so few, here is MY WAY, Jesus was saying, to complete the task.

- *"Pray earnestly"* The first step is to pray. Pray before going. Pray before planning. Do nothing else before you pray! You will be amazed what is happening right now throughout the world in the lives of newly saved disciples of Jesus—before they leave their homes each day, they pray The Harvest Prayer.

- But, notice, this is no casual, cold prayer. It is an earnest, heartfelt prayer. Why should the prayer be earnest? Firstly, because the need of others is so great. They will perish if they die without Christ. And secondly, because of our own tremendous need. It is so easy to be sidetracked from the mission. To get absorbed into the daily grind and forget why we exist. We need God to put us in contact with another person in such a way that it is unmistakable.

When you start your day, do you pray earnestly about anything? We really need help—and that is where the Holy Spirit comes in so effectively. He is our Prayer Helper! Paul encourages us that 'the Spirit helps us in our weakness. For we do not know what to pray for as we ought, but the Spirit himself intercedes for us with groanings too deep for words" (Romans 8:26). That is really intense prayer! Ask the Spirit to help you pray passionately, and He will because that is one of the great duties He lovingly performs in and for us.

Matthew's account of The Harvest Prayer is preceded by these soul-wrenching words describing the heart of Jesus, "When he saw the crowds, he had compassion for them, because they were harassed and helpless, like sheep without a shepherd" (9:36). Harassed and helpless! Is that how we view those around us? Strangers and neighbors? Friends and enemies?

Pray with me now, "Oh, Spirit of God, who filled Jesus so completely, please drain our selfishness and coldness, open our hearts as widely as possible, filling us afresh with divine compassion. And may this mark our 'earnestly' praying The Harvest Prayer each and every day! May our prayer for You to send us and others out into the harvest be set on fire by the deepest desire we are capable of having. Deeper than when we pray for the health of a loved one, the feeding of those starving, the rescue of those facing imminent peril, the provision of a much-needed job, the payment needed for our rent, the revival of our church. May it even equal the groanings we have for the salvation of our own lost children. PLEASE, Holy Spirit, transform our wills, our longings into earnest supplications for the souls and lives of the lost. Make this our greatest craving in life, and so consume us each day as we pray The Harvest Prayer."

• *"to the Lord of the harvest"* Jesus even tells us how to address God in this short, amazing prayer. We are to call Him, *"The Lord of the harvest."* That is, we are to keep in mind that the One to whom we are praying knows who is going to be saved, when they are going to be saved and how they are going to be saved. He is in control. He is the Master, Lord or Overseer of the whole harvest! He, alone, knows what condition each grain is in. Is it green or ripe? Only He knows because it is all His work of grace. If we are praying about reaching others with the gospel and advancing the Kingdom of Christ, it is wonderful to be speaking with the only One in the universe who has that work in His hands!

• *"to send out laborers into his harvest"* Neither God nor we want to waste time. Harvest work is a time-sensitive work. So that we do not go to the wrong place and exert ourselves in fruitless labors, He is willing to place us right into the harvest. He will lead us to those whom He has readied to receive the message! Jesus warned the disciples that unless God does this, a soul cannot be saved. No one can come to me unless the father who sent me draws him" (John 6:44). We should not see our job as chiefly trying to argue others into receptivity. That is His work. He grows the grain and matures it to the harvest stage. We are the reapers!

Is it yet dawning upon your soul just how precious and pivotal The Harvest Prayer is? Some might think this is just "too good to be true." But it isn't. Millions are being saved and discipled by thousands who are praying this prayer each day before they go out into the world. And, now, in a new wave of missionary activity, thousands are praying this prayer before they decide where God is leading them to go as missionaries. We do not want to waste a day in fruitless labor. Missionaries do not want to spend years toiling in the desert when God is willing to send them into the harvest.

A Weak Witness or a Fruitful Discipler?

At this point, I need to ask you a question. "Is it the desire of your heart to fulfill the Great Commission Jesus gave the Church?"

"And Jesus came and said to them, 'All authority in heaven and on earth has been given to me. Go, therefore, and make disciples of all nations, baptizing them in the name of the Father and of the Son and of the Holy Spirit, teaching them to observe (obey) all that I have commanded you. And behold, I am with you always, to the end of the age'" (Matt 28:18-20).

If your answer is, YES, then you need to ask yourselves, "How many disciples have I made?" How many disciples is our church making? Not how many prayers have been prayed. Or how many decisions made with "every head bowed and every eye closed." Not how many Christians we have made who end up going to church and doing little else for Christ. But, how many true disciples have we made who have the marks of a First Century disciple and who make other disciples?[13] How much time and money are we spending outside "the harvest" in weak witnessing efforts that are not making disciples who make disciples?

Before we look at the fruit of those praying The Harvest Prayer today around the globe, we must consider the other pieces of the harvest puzzle. Jesus commanded those He was sending out, first to pray. He even told them what to pray. After praying, what were they to do? Where would their prayer lead them? Hold onto your hats because we are about to get caught up into the powerful, redeeming wind of the Spirit of God, Himself!

Chapter Five
What Follows the Harvest Prayer?

I was so blessed by reading, **_Contagious Disciple Making_**, by the father-son team, David and Paul Watson. The book has an unforgettable beginning.

"'God, I can't plant churches anymore. I didn't sign on to love people, train people, send people, and get them killed.' Six men I had worked with had been martyred over the last eighteen months…. There were 80 million Bhojpuri living in an area known as the 'graveyard of missions and missionaries.' …There were only 27 evangelical churches in the area (of India).

'…Take away my call. I will go back to the States. I'm good at business. I will give lots of money to missions. Let someone else plant churches. Let me go. Release me from my call.'

Every day for two months we had the same conversation. Every day I went to my office, sat in the dark, and begged God to take away my call. And every day He refused.

'Fine… show me in Your Word how You want me to reach these people. If you show me, I will do it.'"[14]

God revealed The Harvest Prayer and its contexts, plus other Gospel texts, to missionary David Watson. And, slowly, he developed a team who began praying and going as Jesus had commanded. To everyone's surprise, this is what happened.

"All of a sudden, we saw 8 churches planted in one year. The next year, there were 48 new churches planted. The year after that, 148, then 327, and then 500. In the fifth year, we saw more than 1,000 new churches planted! …A formal survey of the work among the Bhojpuri showed that our team actually had underreported the number of churches planted in the area! By 2008, another survey of the work revealed 80,000 churches planted and 2 million people baptized"[15]

In this chapter, I want briefly to explore what can happen when the Lord of the harvest answers our prayers and places us into the harvest. This is all anticipated in The Harvest Prayer context of Luke 10:1-20. So, I will continue on in that passage.

Luke 10:3 "Go your way, behold, I am sending you out as lambs in the midst of wolves."

- After the command to pray, comes the command to go. We go daily with faith that the Lord of the harvest will guide us as we go out into the world of business, shopping, recreation, schooling, wherever.
- Jesus reminds us of the hostility of the world in general with the starkest metaphor. Lambs have no chance of surviving among hungry wolves apart from their shepherd. As we are going, we must trust completely in Jesus, the Good Shepherd, protecting and providing for us.

One of the fastest growing areas in the world today, where thousands of new disciples are being made, very surprisingly, is the Islamic nation of Iran! You can see and hear of the amazing DMMs (Disciple Making Movements) occurring there, many led by formerly Islamic women, in the documentary, "Sheep Among Wolves-vol. 2" accessible on YouTube.

Luke 10:4 "Carry no moneybag, no knapsack, no sandals, and greet no one on the road."

- The Lord of the harvest is sending you on a time-sensitive mission. So don't get sidetracked. And don't worry. He assured His disciples that He would literally provide food and shelter, so money did not matter! What, missions without ample monetary preparation? That's right, and to prove that this was the norm, in all the sending outs that Jesus conducted while making disciples, at the end of His life He asked this question in the Upper Room: *"When I sent you out with no moneybag or knapsack or sandals, did you lack anything?" They said, "Nothing" (Luke 22:35).*

So, how does the Lord of the harvest provide for those who leave their homes and loved ones and go into a new context to reap souls? To our thinking, this is impossible. Irrational. Perhaps even irresponsible. But that is the genius of an all-powerful King who loves the world and wants His disciples to reach all nations. He promises to be with us, even to go before and after us. How is this being done today? Just as it was done in Jesus' day.

Luke 10:5-7 "Whatever house you enter, first say, "Peace to this house!" And if a son of peace is there, your peace will rest upon him. But if not, it will return to you. And remain in the same house, eating and drinking what they provide, for the laborer deserves his wages."

- When Jesus told His disciples to do something first, they learned that it was to be done first. Not second or third, and certainly not to be forgotten and disregarded altogether. I have joined the hundreds of thousands of disciples who now enter every place with expectant faith praying, *"peace to this place."*

- This is how you can find the harvest. By obeying the command of Jesus to speak peace as you prayerfully go anywhere. And you will learn to do so expectantly, because He will surprise you by many people of peace responding favorably to your presence.

- *"Your peace will rest on him."* We must be filled with the Spirit, whose fruit is peace, in order to have peace to rest on others. No peace in you will lead to no, or few, people of peace being found. Paul refers to this practice when he listed one piece of our spiritual armor being *"and as shoes for your feet, having put on readiness given by the gospel of peace" (Eph. 6:15).*

- Do you see why they do not have to take their own provisions? The receptive, prepared person of peace will host them, feeding and providing what they need. (See Appendix Two – Receptivity: The Mark of a Person of Peace).

- This way of finding and winning the lost is very different than the pressurized methods of evangelism that I was taught and employed all my life. Peace rather than pressure. Doesn't that sound good to you?

- For the purpose of this small book, that is as far as we will go in examining Luke 10. For those who want more coverage, see Appendix Four: The Rest of the Luke 10 Story.

If this seems too good to be true, I could tell you of scores of accounts that I know of where Luke 10 has and is happening. And some of them are occurring in the most dangerous, anti-Christian places on earth. But let a few suffice.

It is Happening TODAY!

In the collaborative mission effort represented in Trousdale's book, Miraculous Movements, over 100,000 new disciples were made. As they prayed The Harvest Prayer and went where God led, all across sub-Saharan Africa, how many people of peace did they find? Over 18,000 were readied by the Spirit to host the traveling disciple makers! And of these 18,000, more than 20% were the imams of the local mosques! Here is the true story of one of these new disciples led out of Islam by disciple makers who were praying and following The Harvest Prayer.

Sheikh Hanif (not his real name) was a leading Muslim who had been recruited to organize Islamic communities and plant new mosques. Having done this for eight years, there were five voids still deeply hidden in his soul:

"He longed for certainty regarding his status with God. He struggled to find answers or reasons for the violence inside his Islamic world. He grieved at the lack of compassion for suffering people. And recognized that his religion did not allow him or the people he led to make choices for themselves, nor did it give them satisfying answers for the huge struggles of life."[16]

In the midst of his longings for answers, Hanif had a startling dream. In it, Jesus (Isa al Masih in the Quran), appeared to him, identified Himself, and said, "If you obey me, you will succeed in what you have longed for in your life." Then Jesus showed him a tree standing alone on the top of a hill and the face of a man. Hanif knew where the location was, but not the man. Jesus said in the dream, "Go now, and wait under the tree by the road. Look for this man, for he is my servant. You will recognize him when you see him. Find him, for he will show you the true answers to all your questions about God."

You should read the story for yourself because the details are riveting. It ends with Hanif finding the man, being discipled (with his wife) by that Christ follower, and soon becoming a prolific disciple maker and church planter. Jerry ends the story with these words: "The very good news is that every day, hundreds of stories, like Hanif's, are happening throughout the Muslim world."[17]

And this is happening not only in the Muslim world and in India. Even here in the USA there are increasing numbers of us who are following the basic plan of Luke 10. It is quite simple yet has revolutionized the way many of us now do outreach and mission work. In fact, it has become our way of life.

When I make disciples, I normally do not leave my home for a new location. My setting does not exactly parallel that of the 72 Jesus sent out. Neither will yours. We go out for part of the day and return home. But there are four clear steps in the format of Luke 10 that parallels most of our contexts. And here they are:

4 Steps of Jesus' Discipling in Luke 10

1. PRAY
2. GO
3. FIND (people of peace)
4. DISCIPLE

I was in a motel on a Saturday going over my sermon notes for the next day. I was guided by the Spirit to continue down in the lobby of the motel. So, I loaded up my Bible and notes and entered the elevator. On the way down, I prayed, "peace to this place" for the lobby and went into a corner to finish my sermon. Out of nowhere a man walked up to me and asked, "Is that the holy Word of God you are reading?" I knew what was going on, so I replied, "Yes, it is. Are you interested in the Bible?" He was very responsive, so I kept talking. I soon asked him the classic person of peace question: "Would you like to discover for yourself what God is like and how God wants you to live?" I will never forget his response.

He said, "Are you inviting me to a Bible study? I do not want to go to a Bible study and look like a fool because I do not know the Bible well." Many of us use the Discovery Bible Study method (DBS) when discipling. So I assured him, you will never look like a fool in this study because you will not be taught by men, you will be taught by God! And I have trained people in this area, who would gladly meet with you and you will discover from God what He is like and how He wants you to live. Michael (his real name) was all in, gave me his cell number and my two friends began meeting with him in a DBS.[18]

I could go on and on, giving examples of people of peace whom God has connected with Debby and me as we have prayed The Harvest Prayer and then simply gone out into our day speaking peace wherever we enter. We have seen a Chinese scholar, in America studying, discipled in 10 days using DBS! A Jewish woman came over to our table at McDonalds, interrupted my praying with a disciple I was training, and said, "I know you are men of God. You must come over to my table now because I and my mother need your help." A Muslim man came and stood before me at Dunkin Donuts and said, in the hearing of everyone, "I want you to come to my home and teach me the ways of God." A learning- disabled man invited me and a friend into his apartment to disciple him by using Bible pictures and stories. He had a difficult time reading off a page. DBS is perfect for such people as God teaches them through our asking three simple questions of each story!

Debby and I left Philadelphia because we knew we had trained enough disciple makers there. He led us to the largest, super-active 55+ community in Delaware. We have lived here 1.5 years, having known no one here when we came. Simply by praying The Harvest Prayer daily and speaking peace wherever we go, an incredible ministry has developed which, we pray, will impact every county in Delmarva.[19] Won't you join us in following Jesus as obedient, Spirit-filled disciples? The next chapter will hopefully help you start following Him fruitfully today!

Chapter Six
When the Train Hops the Tracks

God, the Lord of the harvest, is "not wishing that any should perish but that all should reach repentance" (2 Pet 3:9). And His great plan of salvation reveals that millions, globally, will become disciples. "After this I looked, and behold, a great multitude that no one could number, from all tribes and peoples and languages, standing before the throne and before the Lamb ... and crying out with a loud voice, 'Salvation belongs to our God who sits on the throne, and to the Lamb!'" (Rev. 7:9-10).

God's plan to redeem this world includes our responsible activity. His plan involves our lives as Jesus invites us to follow Him and become disciple makers. He trained the original disciples, like many rabbis, after a specific model. What is vital for us to understand is that the best model to reach the world is the same today as it was in the First Century. We just need to get back on track with the original. Jesus' plan and promise were, "Follow me, and I will make you fishers of men" (Matt 4:19). Not, "I may make you," but "I will make you." There is fruitfulness, reproduction in following Jesus. And we are being reminded by the faithful witness of thousands globally, that we need to get back to the original. We need a renewal. A returning to when it was NEW. The train hopped the tracks when the original was seriously altered and scrapped.

Many Christians today live in a self-focused, unfruitful way. This is not only wrong, Jesus warned that such selfishness is both perilous to them and to others.[20] He said, "Whoever is not with me (following as a disciple) is against me, and whoever does not gather with me scatters" (Matt 12:30). It should be unthinkable for Christians to keep the Light of the world, the way of salvation, to themselves and allow their neighbors and the nations of the world to die in their sins.

As the great 19th century theologian, Charles Hodge (1797-1878) lamented,

"In the gift of His Son, the revelation of His Word, the mission of the Spirit, and the institution of the Church, God has made abundant provision for the salvation of the world. That the Church has been so remiss in making known the gospel is her guilt. We must not charge the ignorance and consequent perdition of the heathen upon God. The guilt rests on us. We have kept to ourselves the bread of life and allowed the nations to perish...."[21]

We cannot blame God for the eternal death of so many people. Just as there is devastation when a train leaves the tracks, there has been havoc and ruin whenever Christians have stopped following Jesus.

So, this is what we have learned so far. In His training, Jesus personified a life of constant contact (prayer) through the Spirit to the Father. He was the perfect Disciple. The ideal example for us, His disciples. As Peter described Him, "But when you do good and suffer for it you endure, this is a gracious thing in the sight of God. For to this you have been called because Christ also suffered for you, leaving you an example, so that you may follow in his steps" (1 Pet 2:21). He then trained His disciples to trust His leading, as He trusted His Father's leading. Teaching them The Harvest Prayer and the strategy of connecting with people of peace that unfolded from it, was the way that they would go forward and disciple nations.

But, somewhere through the history of the Church, many of His people stopped following Him and His example. They stopped praying The Harvest Prayer and finding people of peace. Instead of making disciples, their attention was taken over by other interests. Rather than being disciples who obeyed their Master, they became Christians who just went to church. They became passive instead of active. Forgetting that Jesus *"has washed us from our sins by His own blood and has made us kings and priests to His God and Father" (Rev 1:5-6-NKJV),* most believers stopped fervently interceding for others and discipling them. The Harvest Prayer and its precious missional strategy were lost. The train tragically hopped the tracks.

There is plenty of blame that could be passed around, involving both personal sin and the Church's agenda over many centuries. But that is not why I am writing. My goal is to encourage and enlighten you, so you can repent and join millions who have gotten back on the tracks!

Back on the Tracks

One way to fix the problem is simply to record how prayer has become a priority in the lives and ministries of today's disciples around the world. The same Holy Spirit that is helping them to pray so sacrificially can begin to do the same in our lives today. If we are willing to listen and repent.

When I was pastoring a church in Philadelphia, we invited Jerry Trousdale, Richard Williams, Dave Hunt and Shodonkeh Johnson to come and train us in DMM and DBS. I will never forget when Shodonkeh taught on prayer. He said, "America will never experience a Disciple Making Movement (DMM) until American Christians learn how to pray." As the host pastor who had focused on prayer, I was a bit offended. I thank God for the loving-yet-bold admonition of my African brother, because it led to the Spirit humbling me and leading me to repent.

How do Shodonkeh and other former Muslims, now disciples of Jesus, pray?

Jerry writes,

"The goal was and continues to be that every new Christian in the DMMs would fast and pray corporately every week, and that every family or individual would invest time every day in prayer and studying God's Word. It was and is of utmost importance…that every person who becomes a follower of Jesus also becomes an intercessor.…

"Weekly days of fasting and prayer have become an integral part of the normal Christian life, and most of their members spend 2-4 nights a month in half-night prayer meetings."[22]

When these new disciples pray The Harvest Prayer, seeking the Lord to literally guide them into an entirely new territory, their prayers are anything but superficial. Again Jerry notes,

"Some believers fast during daylight hours, only eating small meals in the evenings and taking breaks on Saturdays, and they continue that discipline for an entire month prior to taking the gospel to a new area."[23]

So, praying The Harvest Prayer is not a once-off "saying the right words." Jesus commanded "pray earnestly." The Harvest Prayer is a matter of life and death. And when the disciple gets

THAT, passion follows. James reminded us, "The effective, fervent prayer of a righteous man avails much" (James 5:16b-NKJV). Whether it is for daily guidance into the harvest around us or for direction to a new field of harvest, The Harvest Prayer is always a fervent expression of deep, agape love.

Two more accounts will suffice to flesh-out what Shodonkeh meant when he called us as American Christians to learn again what it means to pray. Or, as Paul commanded the Colossians, "Devote yourselves to prayer, being watchful and thankful" (Col 4:3).The following examples have made me pause and reflect whether I even understand what Paul meant when he said to all of his church plants and colleagues, "For God is my witness, whom I serve with my spirit in the gospel of his Son, that without ceasing I mention you always in my prayers" (Rom 1:9-10; Eph 1:16; 1 Thes 1:2; 2 Tim 1:3; Phile 4, etc). My training for the ministry and my mentors in the ministry did not emphasize prayer in the way the New Testament does. Many of us have had a virtually prayerless ministry compared to the disciples of the 1st and 21st centuries!

Trousdale introduces us to the life and ministry of one prayer warrior with these words,

"By any measure, Mama Nadirah (not her name) was an extraordinary woman. She had grown up in a Muslim home where she was grounded in the Qur'an... unfortunately her background did not include a chance for girls to have any formal education, and Nadirah never had the opportunity to learn how to read or write.... God's hand had brought her together with a Christian named Charles, leading her to a happy marriage and to exposure to Jesus the Messiah. Sadly, after many years of marriage and raising a family … Charles died. Yet Nadirah discovered that, even in her sorrow, she was not alone; she found that she had the Holy Spirit of God to guide and strengthen her, and she discovered the power of prayer….

"Over time, Nadirah (still illiterate, but having memorized many Bible stories) began to pray with a new level of faith, and then with fervent prayer, prayer with fasting, and even all-night prayers. She lived to pray and to introduce her friends to a life in the presence of God, coaching and mentoring them in the process. Despite the disadvantage of not being lettered, Nadirah took all the training she could get in prayer, disciple making and church planting, and she excelled. She opened her home and her heart to anyone who came in need of prayer, counsel, friendship, or simply a hot meal."[24]

Mama Nadirah has seen God so bless her prayer ministry, that she "has seen a harvest of more than 200,000 new Christians in seven years!"[25] God, raise up Mama Nadirah's in the USA, so the great multiplying work of DMMs may begin!

David Watson further challenges us in the West (or Global North) by writing about the prime importance of prayer in the most fruitful disciple makers he knows.

"In a meeting of the top 100 disciple-makers in our ministry, we looked for common elements among these high-producing leaders. Each of these disciple-makers, along with the teams they led, started more than 20 churches per year. One group started more than 500 churches in the previous year. We found many common elements among the different groups, but the only element that was present in every team was a high commitment to prayer. These leaders spent an average of 3 hours per day in personal prayer. They spent another 3 hours in prayer with their teams every day…. They also spent one day per week in fasting and prayer. The whole team spent one weekend per month in fasting and prayer."[26]

As you pick your jaw off the floor, just be encouraged. Like babies, we have to begin to crawl before we can walk or run. My research and experience have led me to conclude that most prayer warriors and groups *begin* with a small group meeting to pray one hour per week. God will bless your starting!

Following the lead of Jesus, together with both 1st century and 21st century disciples, we make the establishing of DMM Prayer Groups the first step towards seeing a biblical renewal of discipleship in any home, church or region. Harvest praying precedes harvest going and harvest reaping.

Watson concluded, "As we started looking at Disciple-Making Movements worldwide, we made a critical observation: a prayer movement precedes every Disciple-Making Movement."[27]

The only power that can birth such prayer is the power of the Holy Spirit, who is referred to in the following: "Now to him who is able to do far more abundantly than all that we ask or think, **according to the power at work within us**, to him be glory in the church…." (Eph 3:20).

Once the Spirit fills us, we will be filled with divine love. We will then love God with all our heart and desire to communicate with Him in prayer. So, may your renewal begin as you obey the apostolic command of submitting yourself completely to 'be filled with the Spirit" (Eph 5:18). This is the only way we know of how that train can get placed back onto the tracks. God must do the big lifting. With us, alone, it is impossible. But not with God. With God all things are possible!

Chapter Seven
Why NO DMMs in the USA?

A Disciple Making Movement (DMM) is defined as 1000 new disciples and, thereby, many new church plants made in one region, over a short period of time by up to four generations of disciple makers. Glenn Sunshine, Jerry Trousdale and Greg Benoit wrote an article this month in The Christian Post where they affirmed, "Across Africa and Asia, millions of people in historically unengaged people groups are now in rapidly growing Disciple Making Movements. In 2000 there were 6 such movements, today there are now 1,035![28]

Let that sink in. Only 6 DMMs existed in 2000 and now there are at least 1,035 DMMs. These are trackable, significant movements. The Holy Spirit is working in some places in an unparalleled way-TODAY. The article continues,

- Almost all of the Pygmy peoples of Africa are seeing dramatic transformation by the Gospel of the Kingdom in the last 12 years.[29]
- Hundreds of large people groups that had been Muslim for many centuries, are now seeing ordinary people making disciples that transform whole communities.
- Across Africa and Asia many thousands of former Muslim clerics have left Islam to become fearless disciples of Christ.

These men, writing in an American newspaper, wondered why our country is being passed over by this great renewal. They remarked,

"We are living in a season of the greatest church growth since the 1st century! But half of the world is missing the move of God. How is it possible that the Global South Church is seeing Christian history being made while the Global North church is struggling for answers? God alone provides the increase, but why there and not here?"[30]

After 5 years of studying the differences between churches involved in DMMs and those not experiencing them[31], these researchers noted that the top differences were:

1. Abundant, bold prayer

2. Discipling to Conversion

3. Obedience-based Discipleship

4. Empowering ordinary people for ministry

5. Make replicating disciples, not converts

6. Never-ending leadership training for all[32]

You can read about all of these areas in the indispensable book based on their research, *The Kingdom Unleashed*. I am concerned now only with the number one difference they mentioned – PRAYER. Because, as we have demonstrated, this is the matter of main importance to Jesus. Without the first command being obeyed, the remaining promises will not be fulfilled. Where there is ignorance of The Harvest Prayer, there are no Disciple Making Movements!

A very important joint study between Discipleship.org and Exponential.org, in partnership with some 25 other groups, was made public this month. It is entitled, **National Study on**

Disciple Making Churches in the USA: *High Aspirations Amidst Disappointing Results*. They concluded that less than 5% of American churches were characterized as growing churches who were "reproducing disciples and disciple making." This study concluded that they had found no churches in the USA who were "multiplying disciples and disciple making." Some churches in the USA are **adding** but where are the churches where disciples are **multiplying** into an undeniable, unstoppable movement?

There is a reason why Luke summarized the exponential growth of the Jerusalem church in Acts with these words, "And the word of God continued to increase, and the number of disciples **multiplied greatly** in Jerusalem, and a great many of the priests became obedient to the faith" (Acts 6:7). Judea was experiencing a Disciple Making Movement, which even horrendous persecution could not stop.

"And there arose on that day a great persecution against the church in Jerusalem, and they were all scattered throughout the regions of Judea and Samaria, except the apostles.… Now those who were scattered went about preaching the word" (Acts 8:1, 4).

Exponential multiplication is the evidence of a Disciple Making Movement. And all recorded DMMs begin with a DMM prayer focus. At the foundation of DMM prayer is a living faith in and praying of The Harvest Prayer.

The answer to the question, "Why no DMMs in the USA?" is clearly this:

The Underlying Problems

1. We American Christians must repent of not being disciples who follow Jesus and obey what He has commanded, especially concerning prayer and discipling others.

2. We must trust in the whole gospel. Our repentance and lives must be gospel-soaked! The call by Jesus has always been, "Repent and believe the gospel" (Mark 1:15). The gospel gives us the twin gifts of God's forgiveness of our sins and Christ's righteousness covering our sins! We are both washed in His blood and wrapped in His perfect obedience! We must be careful about emphasizing the forgiveness of sins while we ignore the equally precious gift of receiving Christ's righteousness. Both are true and neither should be forgotten. Faith in this full gospel, alone, equips us to follow Jesus. When we fall, we do not stay down, because the Spirit reminds us— the One you are with is your perfect Savior. You are accepted "in Him," not apart from Him. That is why John described our walk with Jesus as a fellowship that confesses our sins and is being constantly renewed in forgiveness and power (1 John 1:5-10).

3. We must every day, deny and die to ourselves. Repentance is a daily reality. And it is proven by a renewed life. Or as John the Baptist preached, "bear fruit in keeping with repentance." (Matt 3:8). This is the condition of discipleship. "If anyone would come after me, let him deny himself and take up his cross and follow me. For whoever would save his life will lose it, but whoever loses his life for my sake will save it" (Luke 9:23-24).

4. We must emerge from our daily death to sin, in the power or filling of the Holy Spirit. It is only in the power of the Spirit

that we can follow Jesus, pray without ceasing and go out making disciples. This filling of the Spirit is our responsibility (Eph. 5:18). And it is Jesus' promise, "If you then who are evil know how to give good gifts to your children, how much more will the heavenly Father give the Holy Spirit to those who ask him!" (Luke 11:13). The empowering of the Spirit is what daily transformed the early disciples from being merely "uneducated, common men" (Acts 4:13) to being "mighty in God for pulling down strongholds" (2 Cor. 10:4)!

5. We must submit to Jesus in radically simple, immediate obedience, following Him and doing His will just as we would if He were physically present. Because He never leaves nor forsakes us. Joyful obedience, out of love, is the hallmark of true discipleship. And this obedience will lead to being constantly filled with the love and Spirit of God. Even when mistreated, opposed and persecuted. The Apostles boldly affirmed, "And we are witnesses to these things, **and so is the Holy Spirit, whom God has given to those who obey him**" (Acts 5:32).

The Specific Problem – Getting Started

We are all called to "go and make disciples," thus fulfilling Christ's Great Commission. And we have now learned to go, as the early disciples went, following Luke 10:

1. Praying the Harvest Prayer

2. Going into the world

3. Finding people of peace

4. Discipling them in the name of Jesus[33]

For the going, finding and discipling steps, there are many helpful books and videos that you can access even beyond those I have recommended.[34] But there are precious few books that strongly advocate for prayer being first and foremost. That is partially because most discipling books have been written by Westerners who know little of prayer. Certainly, the best way to learn is simply by doing it. Get a partner and start praying The Harvest Prayer. Here's how you can break the prayer down into its parts and pray for each element:

Praying from God's Name as "Lord of the Harvest"

-Adoring the Trinity as Sovereign, in complete control of the process of salvation/harvesting

-Worship God as a Persons of infinite love, who deeply desire a relationship of love and intimacy with all people

Praying from God's "sending out"

-Ask Jesus to reinforce in you the conviction of being sent, with all His authority. (See Romans 10:15!)

-Ask the Spirit to give you assurance to set aside any intimidation, filling you with His power to speak in love (Acts 1:8).

Praying from Jesus making you and other "laborers"

-Request Jesus, by the guidance of the Spirit, to direct your mind, emotions and path into a real harvesting mode.

-Ask the Holy Spirit to teach you how to best work the harvest and, so, become an adept laborer in the harvest work.

Praying from the Spirit guiding you "into the harvest"

-Give your daily schedule and entire life to God, so you are ready to enter the harvest at any minute and through all means.

-Ask the Spirit to fill you with His love, so that there is no part of the harvest that you are unwilling or hesitant to enter.

-Tell Jesus that you really want to follow Him so He can make you a real fisher of men. It is His promise—so let Him know that you want Him to be successful in transforming your life into a successful disciple maker or harvester.

We have also learned, from Dave and Paul Watson to pray through the parables of the Kingdom as a good way of Harvest Praying. (See Appendix Seven, **Praying through the Kingdom Parables**, where I explain how to do this in your DMM Prayer times.)

It is vital that you read Luke 10 as a disciple would have heard it. They would have memorized it and followed it in exact order. So, once you pray and set out on your day, you should be expectant, as Peter said, *"Always be prepared to give an answer to everyone who asks you to give the reason for the hope that you have. But do this with gentleness and respect" (1 Pet 3:15)*. Generally expectant. And specifically, ready for any specific person or context that the Spirit might have put in your mind or heart when you prayed. But, as Peter noted, there should be no pressure, only peace, gentleness and respect. Harvesting is essentially God's work. There are many times when the apples will just fall off the tree at your feet. People of peace will sometimes find you, instead of you finding them.

My prayer for you is that each of you will prove to be a real disciple, Christ's "good soil" who has "heard the word and understands it… and bears fruit and yields, in one case one hundred fold, in another sixty and in another thirty" (Matt 13:23). This will all begin with prayer, or you may be sowing your seed only on infertile or unfruitful soil. Praying the Harvest Prayer is Jesus' way to assure you that you will not waste your time and effort.

Can you give a good reason why DMMs should not be emerging in the USA? It is just up to us to follow Jesus as He intended and as our brothers and sisters are doing globally. I pray that this little book may be used in your life and in our world in a big way—for the glory of Jesus and the advancement of His Kingdom!

"But you, beloved, building yourselves up in your most holy faith and praying in the Holy Spirit, keep yourselves in the love of God, waiting for the mercy of our Lord Jesus Christ that leads to eternal life." (Jude 20-21[35])

Appendix One
Jesus' Seven Invitations to Pray (John 14-16)

In one setting, the Upper Room, over a space of a few hours, when meeting for the last time with His disciples prior to His betrayal and death, Jesus focused seven times on prayer. At no other time did Jesus emphasize one thing so much. And no other moment, for His Apostles, was as intimate and precious as this. Carefully meditate on these verses, and let the priority of prayer, which Jesus obviously wanted to establish in their lives, arise to a true devotion in your life.

The seven invitations to pray are launched by one of the most remarkable promises Jesus ever spoke, "Truly, truly I say to you, whoever believes in me will do the works that I do; and greater works than these will he do, because I am going to the Father" (John 14:12). Most Christians are so surprised and confused by this statement that they fail to realize that Jesus, in the very next two things He said, explained HOW this would happen—through prayer! The seven invitations to prayer, loaded with unbelievable promises, flow from the declaration that His disciples would do even greater things than He did! How can this be? PRAYER!

1. "Whatever you ask in my name, this I will do, that the Father may be glorified in the Son." (John 14:13)

2. "If you ask me anything in my name, I will do it." (John 14:14)

3. "If you abide in me, and my words abide in you, ask whatever you wish, and it will be done for you." (John 15:7)

4. "You did not choose me, but I chose you and appointed you that you should go and bear fruit and that your fruit should abide, so that whatever you ask the Father in my name, he may give it to you." (John 15:16)

5. "In that day you will ask nothing of me. Truly, truly I say to you, whatever you ask of the Father in my name, he will give it to you." (John 16:23)

6. "Until now you have asked nothing in my name. Ask, and you will receive, that your joy may be full." (John 16:24)

7. In that day you will ask in my name, and I do not say to you that I will ask the Father on your behalf; for the Father himself loves you, because you have loved me and have believed that I came from God." (John 16:26-27)

I share these in their sheer and profound simplicity, so that you can bathe your souls in them and come to embrace them by faith. Sometime, you may want to read the simple answer I give to the question, "Why most Christians' Prayers are NOT Answered"[36]

Appendix Two
Who were the 72?

The Gospels clearly reveal the origin of the Twelve Apostles. Mark wrote,

"And he went up on the mountain and called to him those whom he desired, and they came to him. And he appointed twelve (whom he also named apostles) so that they might be with him and he might send them out to preach and have authority to cast out demons. He appointed them twelve: Simon (to whom he gave the name Peter); James the son of Zebedee and John the brother of James (to whom he gave the name Boanerges, that is, Sons of Thunder); Andrew, and Philip, and Bartholomew, and Matthew, and Thomas, and James the son of Alphaeus, and Thaddaeus, and Simon the Zealot, and Judas Iscariot, who betrayed him" (Mark 3:13-19).

The Twelve are listed in three other texts (Matt 10:2-4; Luke 6:14-16; Acts 1:13). Luke's account is similar to Mark's, except that Luke mentions that Jesus *"went out to the mountain to pray, and all night he continued in prayer to God" (Lk 6:12).* Luke notes that the Twelve were selected *"from the disciples." (6:13).* Mark simply says that Jesus *"called to him those whom he desired" (3:13).* So, it is evident that the Apostles were first, His disciples. It is interesting that John, writing later than the other Gospel authors, never uses the word "apostle," but throughout His account only refers to the Apostles as disciples. He does call them "the Twelve" once in 20:24.

The Apostles were sent out on a special training mission in Matt. 10:1-15. When they are listed by Matthew, they are put in pairs. Peter and Andrew, James and John, Philip and Bartholomew, Thomas and Matthew, James and Thaddaeus,

Simon the Zealot and Judas Iscariot. This sending out "two by two" became a feature of Jesus' sendings. Mark 6 refers to a time when *"Calling out the Twelve to him, he sent them out two by two and gave them authority over evil spirits" (6:7).*

We have seen that when Jesus sent out the 72, He sent them *"two by two into every town and place where he himself was about to go."* The reason He sent them out two by two is never specifically stated. There were probably several reasons. In the NIV Study Bible, Lewis Foster suggests, "The purpose of going in pairs may have been to bolster credibility by having the testimony of more than one witness (cf. Deut 17:6), as well as to provide mutual support during their training period."[37] Whatever the reasons, the Apostles knew it was important. So, the first official action they performed, after Jesus ascended into heaven, was to prayerfully select another apostle to take the place of Judas Iscariot. This would have been especially necessary if the Apostles saw themselves as ministering in pairs. Prior to the casting of the lots to determine between Barsabbas and Matthias, they prayed, *"You, Lord, who know the hearts of all, show which one of these two you have chosen to take place in this ministry and apostleship from which Judas turned aside to go to his own place" (Acts 1:24-25).* Luke adds, *"And they cast lots for them, and the lot fell on Matthias, and he was numbered with the eleven apostles" (1:26).*

I believe that all of this is helpful in determining who the 72 were. They were not the apostles but were described simply as *"seventy-two others" (Luke 10:1).* Isn't it precious that the privilege of praying The Harvest Prayer and going out to make disciples is here granted to a large, nameless group of 36 pairs of disciples. And with that simple truth, I believe we have a great clue as to the identity of the 72.

The Twelve Apostles were formed by Jesus into 6 partners or pairs. They labored in this way and it just felt wrong to them to leave one apostle hanging without a partner, so the Lord chose Matthias. If the Twelve, in their training period, did to others what Jesus has done to them, how many carefully trained disciples would have been made or produced? Jesus chose 12. If each of the 6 groups discipled the same number as Jesus chose to disciple, the result would be 72. 6 x 12=72.

Understanding just how carefully disciples would follow or imitate their Rabbi, it would not surprise me if the 72 were simply the disciples who were made by the Apostles. I cannot prove this because it is not clearly stated in the Word. But, for me, it is as good an explanation of the Scriptural data as any other. And there have been many who believe that the number 12 seems significant and have found great fruitfulness in discipling twelve others. Dr. Joel Comiskey has authored two books focusing on "Groups of 12," and the G 12 Church Movement[38]

Appendix Three
Receptivity: The Mark of a Person of Peace

How will you know when you encounter a person of peace? There are several ways to "test the soil." But the chief, biblical way is simply to assess if the person is truly receptive to you and to your desire to help and share the Word with him/her.

In Luke 10, the person of peace is a hospitable host. John broad brushed true believers as follows: "But to all who did receive him, who believed in his name, he gave the right to become children of God" (John 1:12). "Receive" here is the normal word for taking someone home with you. Of letting Jesus into the intimate matters of their lives.

In the brilliant training passage of Matt. 10, Jesus summarizes the terms of discipleship in this way:

"Whoever loves father or mother more than me is not worthy of me, and whoever loves son or daughter more than me is not worthy of me. And whoever does not take his cross and follow me is not worthy of me. Whoever finds his life will lose it, and whoever loses his life for my sake will find it. Whoever receives you, receives me, and whoever receives me receives him who sent me. The one who receives a prophet because he is a prophet will receive a prophet's reward, and the one who receives a righteous person because he is a righteous person will receive a righteous person's reward. And whoever gives one of these little ones a cup of cold water because he (the young one) is a disciple, truly, I say to you, he will by no means lose his reward" (Matt. 10:37-42).

Notice the emphasis on receptivity in the last verses. Helpfully, the giving of a cup of cold water is substituted for "receives" in v 42. This shows that receptivity reveals a willingness to provide for or help the discipler.

The Thessalonian church is uniquely set apart by Paul as his most ideal church plant.[39] Receptivity, the first mark of their being people of peace, is listed by Paul with other notable characteristics they possessed,

"For not only has the word of the Lord sounded forth from you in Macedonia and Achaia, but your faith in God has gone forth everywhere, so that we need not say anything. For they themselves (the pagans) report concerning us the kind of reception we had among you, and how you turned to God from idols to serve the living and true God, and to wait for his Son from heaven…." (1 Thess 1:7-10).

This could easily be overlooked as irrelevant by anyone who is not familiar with the requirement by Jesus that a person of peace be receptive. Phil Alessi has written a very helpful booklet on identifying people of peace.[40] And global disciplers often ask a simple "person of peace" question (PoP question). Which aims at starting a DBS with the receptive person or group.[41]

Instead of making this too long, you could simply work your way through the Book of Acts and list the people of peace there. You will find many. Take Lydia for example:

"One who heard us was a woman named Lydia… The Lord opened her heart to pay attention to what was said by Paul. And after she was baptized… she urged us, saying, 'If you have judged me to be faithful to the Lord, come to my house and stay.' And she prevailed upon us." (Acts 16:14-15).

Her receptivity was both a spiritual and physical characteristic of her life.

In Luke 10, the person of peace receives, giving room and board to the discipling team. On the contrary, if the disciples do not find people of peace, but instead, rejectors, they are to wipe the dust of their feet off as a witness against them (Luke 10:11; see also Matt 10:14 and Mark 6:11). I find it both fascinating and illustrative that Paul's missionary team did the same thing in cities and to people who did not well-receive them (Acts 13:51; 18:6). The model of Jesus was perpetuated by His disciples for many generations.

As Paul reminisced late in his life when writing to Timothy, "What you have heard from me in the presence of many witnesses entrust to faithful men who will be able to teach others also" (2 Tim 2:2). Note, that there are four generations of discipling going on. There is no indication by Paul that alteration or improvements in the form of discipling were ever to be in view. The high-water mark was Jesus. The cornerstone was Jesus. He is the Alpha and the Omega. What He passes on and how He passes it on is to be the norm. Paul implied this when he wrote to the Corinthians, in the midst of their rebellion, "For I received from the Lord what I also delivered to you...." (1 Cor 11:23). When did he receive anything from the Lord? He gives his answer to the Galatians,

"For I would have you know, brothers, that the gospel that was preached by me is not man's gospel. For I did not receive it from any man , nor was I taught it, but I received it through a revelation of Jesus Christ... nor did I go up to Jerusalem to those who were apostles before me, but I went away into Arabia…." (Gal 1:11,12,17).

Paul was taught, somehow, by Jesus. The form and the content of his discipleship would have followed Jesus so closely that he could command, "Be imitators of me, as I am of Christ" (1 Cor. 11:1).

All you have to do is watch Paul's form and you will see Christ's form. Go first to the synagogue until they reject you. Then move out from there. Jesus went to reach the common Jew in the open air. Paul went to the Gentiles. Jesus healed the receptive and so did Paul. Is there any instance of Jesus or His apostles healing a live person who did not want to be healed?

Salvation is God's shalom—His peace. Jesus was "the son of David," epitomized best by Solomon—whose name is akin to shalom. The Prince of peace will subdue and rule by peace. "Come to me, all who labor and are heavy laden, and I will give you rest. Take my yoke upon you, and learn from me, for I am gentle and lowly in heart, and you will find rest for your souls. For my yoke is easy and my burden is light" (Matt 11:28-30). Rabbis in Jesus' day would often call their disciples into a discipling relationship with the words, "take my yoke on you." Gentle, meek, peaceful Savior. When and where He reigns, the lion will lay down with the lamb.

So, it is today. Even when writing to the disciples in the center of the idolatrous Roman empire, governed by a rival god-King, like Nero, Paul assures the vulnerable Church in Rome, "The God of peace will soon crush Satan under your feet" (Rom 16:20)!

Appendix Four
The Rest of the Luke 10 Story

*With special notice of the healing mentioned

Here are some thoughts that flow from the rest of Luke 10.

Luke 10:7a – As long as the person of peace offers hospitality, the missionary stays. This is why they are told not to take money or provisions for themselves on the mission—Christ will prepare the way ahead. He will open hearts. He loves both the seeking sinner and the needy saint. See Luke 22:35.

Luke 10:7b – Note the command not to go "from house to house." This is certainly great counsel when sowing in a resistant region or culture. But it may also be more helpful than Westerners feel in the normal sowing of the gospel. We always need to bear in mind that it is NOT in the number of contacts we make, that we hope for fruit. It is in praying The Harvest Prayer and in finding people of peace. We need to spend more time not less with those who are open and receptive to us and our message. Rushing someone into a profession of faith is not the picture we see here.

This must not be taken as being critical of a "door to door" approach in a free and democratic land. We should use our freedom to go and make disciples. But, I hope, those zealous to evangelize will always understand that God has given us two ways to reach the world: Share the gospel and make disciples. It is not only, "Preach the gospel." Love will allow you to put yourself in their place and discern, "when is the best time to share the truth." "Be wise as serpents and innocent as doves," was a command given in the context of going out on a mission trip. The indiscriminate sharing of truth may be counterproductive. See Matt 10:16ff.

Luke 10:8-9a – This part of the sending instructions, unfortunately, "convinces" some Christians that Luke 10 is NOT for us today. Simply because it says, "Heal the sick in it." And any form of healing ministry is seen, by some, to be limited to earlier times. As in all controversies over biblical texts, it is important to get the whole picture and read the whole revelation. Notice that the healing is preceded by these words, "Whenever you enter a town <u>and they receive you</u>, eat what is set before you. Heal the sick..." In other words, receptivity precedes and confines the healing ministry. This is not a general "healing campaign;" but it is a way to respond, in a receptive context, when sickness is hindering the discipling work.

I have no hesitancy to pray for healing in the life of someone who wants to serve Jesus in discipling others but finds a health condition standing in the way. Debby and I, together and separately, have seen God often heal in such a context. And it is important here to introduce what is said by the returning 72 in v. 17, The seventy-two returned with joy, saying, 'Lord, even the demons are subject to us <u>in your name</u>!'" One would not know that their healing ministry had been carried out "in the name of Jesus," without this added revelation. That is a basic rule in this and our mission and evangelism efforts. What we do is NOT self-empowered but derived from the power of Jesus. It is for the exaltation of Jesus and the advancement of His Kingdom.

I believe that the healing of the 72 was, most definitely, not the result of some "gift of healing" that they had all been given. It was, rather, the fruit of a healing prayer ministry. And, just as stipulated elsewhere, our prayers are all to be expressed "in Jesus' name." That is, with faith in His presence and solely for His glory and the advancement of His Kingdom. That is what praying in Jesus' name means.

This view is further supported by the incident recorded in Mark 9:14-29, where 9 of the Apostles could not deliver a boy from his demonic state. Later, they asked Jesus why this was the case. His response was, This kind (of demon) can come out only by prayer (and fasting-some manuscripts)." Jesus thereby taught that prayer was the greatest power in the healing of others. And this lesson was well-learned by His disciples. In Acts and throughout the rest of the New Testament, we see both the limited "gift of healing" possessed by a very few; but we also see the great power of prayer exercised by all believing disciples.

The support for this view of Luke 10 is being corroborated globally by the amazing miracles of healing and deliverence occurring wherever the gospel is being greatly advanced and disciples are being made. The evidence is, at this point, indisputable among those who are willing to openly research and verify the growing testimonies of disciples globally.[42]

Luke 10:9b – That disciples should remind hearers *"the kingdom of God has come near,"* is very informative. How has the kingdom come near? Through the witness and life of the discipler. We embody the Kingdom of God! His rule is within us and we have joyfully submitted ourselves to Jesus and to His rule. You, dear reader, must take away from this that you are far more important in any context than you probably think. You are the light of the world and the salt of the earth (Matt 5:13,14). Let your light shine, especially to those seeking its light!

Luke 10:10-12 – The pronouncing of judgment on those who refuse the disciple and his/her message is also important. It is not to be done in a stern, rebuking way. But in tenderness and tearfulness which we see flowing from Jesus and the rest of the New Covenant (Testament) witness. Sometimes just the somber mention of consequences for rejecting Jesus and His truth leads to repentance. As mentioned in Appendix 3, Paul and his mission team would routinely wipe the dust off their shoes and coats as a witness against the rejection of the gospel (see Acts 13:51; 18:6).

Luke 10:13-16 – The shame and judgment of those rejecting Jesus and the gospel is here heightened by expressing that their penalty will exceed that delivered to ignorant pagan cities. And the inextricable bond between Father and Son and disciple is highlighted in the words, *"The one who hears you, hears me, and the one who rejects me rejects him who sent me."* Again, dear one, do not underestimate the importance of both you and your mission.

Luke 10:17-20 – It has been said that believers "are immortal until their work is done." This is true of every disciple who goes out and makes disciples. God will protect and provide, even miraculously, for such ones. And the disciple is reminded that the gift of salvation is more precious than all the power in the world. We must remain humble, whatever fruit we are able to produce, because it is all of grace!

Luke 10:21-24 – A special scene of prayer by Jesus, with incredibly touching words, is followed by a final reminder to disciples just how privileged they are (and we are) to be used in the advancement of His Kingdom in such significant ways. God be praised! Come, Lord Jesus!

Appendix Five
Helpful Quotes on Prayer

Thomas a Kempis (1380-1471) "The Imitation of Christ"

1. The saints and friends of Christ served the Lord in hunger and thirst, in cold and nakedness, in work and fatigue, in vigils and fasts, in prayers and holy meditations, in persecutions and many afflictions. How many and severe were the trials they suffered—the Apostles, martyrs, confessors, virgins, and all the rest who willed to follow in the footsteps of Christ! They hated their lives on earth that they might have life in eternity. (chap 18)

Anonymous – The Kneeling Christian

1. Our blessed Lord did not pray simply as an example to us: He never did things merely as an example. He prayed because He needed to pray. As perfect Man, prayer to Him was a necessity. Then how much more is it a necessity to you and me? (14)

2. To God your every want,
    In instant prayer display.
    Pray always; pray and never faint.
    Pray! Without ceasing, pray. (15)

3. When the Revival in Wales was at its height, a Welsh missionary wrote home begging the people to pray that India might be moved in like manner. So the coal miners met daily at the pit-mouth half an hour before dawn to pray for their comrade overseas. In a few weeks' time the welcome message was sent home. "The blessing has come." (18)

4. Many Christians do not give God a chance to show His delight in granting His children's petitions; for their requests are so vague and indefinite. (26) Fellow-Christian, you believe in God, and you believe on Him (John 3:16), but have you advanced far enough in the Christian life to believe Him; that is, to believe what He says and all He says? Does it not sound blasphemous to ask such a thing of a Christian man? Yet how few believers really believe God! God forgive us! Has it ever struck you that we trust the word of our fellowman more easily than we trust God's word? (29)

5. He says, ask "anything," "whatsoever," "what you will," and it shall be done. But then He puts in a qualifying phrase. He says that we are to ask in His name. That is the condition, and the only one, although … it is sometimes couched in different words. If, therefore, we ask and do not receive, it can only be that we are not fulfilling the condition. (41)

6. When we confess that we "never get answers to our prayers," we are not condemning God, or His promises, or the power of prayer, but ourselves. There is no greater test of spirituality than prayer…. "In His name" must be "according to His will." …We must not expect God to reveal His will to us unless we desire to know that will and intend to do that will. Knowledge of God's will and the performance of that will go together… (John 7:17). (47)

7. Prayer is not given us as a burden to be borne, or an irksome duty to fulfil, but to be a joy and power to which there is no limit. (49)

8. How hard the devil makes it for us to concentrate our thoughts upon God! …It is the evil one's chief aim to make prayer impossible. (52)

9. Spurgeon once said, "There is no need for us to go beating about the bush, and not telling the Lord distinctly what it is that we crave at His hands…. I believe in business prayers. I mean prayers in which you take to God one of the many promises which he has given us in His Word, and expect it to be fulfilled as certainly as we look for the money to be given us when we go to the bank to cash a check." (53-54)

10. If we really loved our blessed Savior, should we not oftener seek communion with Him in prayer? (68)

Brother Lawrence (aka Nicholas Herman- 17th Century) - The Practice of the Presence of God

1. Having found in many books different methods of going to God, and divers practices of the spiritual life, I thought this would serve rather to puzzle me than to facilitate what I sought after, which was nothing but how to become wholly God's. (1st Letter).

2. …I renounced, for the love of Him, everything that was not He, and I began to live as if there was none but He and I in the world…. I made this my business as much all the day long as at the appointed times of prayer; for at all times, every hour, every minute, even in the height of my business, I drove away from my mind everything that was capable of interrupting my thought of God. (1st Letter)

3. I have not followed all these methods. On the contrary … I found they discouraged me. This was the reason why, at my entrance into religion, I took a resolution to give myself up to God, as the best return I could make for His love, and, out of love of Him, to renounce all besides. (2nd Letter)

4. I make it my business only to persevere in His holy presence, wherein I keep myself by a simple attention, and a general fond regard to God, which I may call an actual presence of God; or, to speak better, an habitual, silent, and secret conversation of the soul with God, which often causes me joys…inwardly…so great that I am forced to use means to moderate them and prevent their appearance to others. (2ⁿᵈ Letter)

5. As for my set hours of prayer, they are only a continuation of the same exercise. Sometimes I consider myself there as a stone before a carver, whereof he is to make a statue; presenting myself thus before God, I desire Him to form His perfect image in my soul and make me entirely like Himself. (2ⁿᵈ Letter)

6. I know that for the right practice of it, the heart must be empty of all other things, because God will possess the heart alone; and as He cannot possess it alone without emptying it of all besides, so neither can He act there, and do in it what He pleases, unless it be left vacant to Him. (5ᵗʰ Letter)

7. There is not in the world a kind of life more sweet and delightful than that of a continual conversation with God. (5ᵗʰ Letter)

8. Were I a preacher, I should, above all other things, preach the practice of the presence of God. (6ᵗʰ Letter)

9. Our mind is extremely roving; but, at the will is mistress of all our faculties, she must recall them, and carry them to God as their last end. When the mind…has contracted certain bad habits of wandering and dissipation, they are difficult to overcome, and commonly draw us, even against our wills, to the things of the earth. I believe one remedy for this is to confess

our faults and to humble ourselves before God. I do not advise you to use multiplicity of words in prayer, many words and long discourses being often the occasions of wandering. Hold yourself in prayer before God like a dumb or paralytic beggar as a rich man's gate. Let it be your business to keep your mind in the presence of the Lord. (8th Letter)

10. We cannot escape the dangers which abound in life without the actual and continual help of God. Let us, then, pray to Him for it continually. How can we pray to Him without being with Him? How can we be with Him without thinking of Him often? And how can we often think about Him but by a holy habit which we should form of it? You will tell me that I am always saying the same thing. It is true, for this is the best and easiest method I know; and as I use no other, I advise all the world to do it. We must know before we can love. (9th Letter)

11. In order to know God, we must think of Him often; and when we come to love Him, we shall also think of Him often, for our heart wills to be with its treasure. (9th Letter)

12. Pray remember what I have recommended to you, which is, to think often on God, by day, by night, in your business, and even in your diversions. He is always near you and with you; leave Him not alone. You would think it rude to leave a friend alone who came to visit you; why then, must God be neglected? Do not, then, forget Him, but think on Him often, adore Him continually, live and die with Him; this is the glorious employment of a Christian. In a word, this is our profession; if we do not know it, we must learn it. (10th Letter)

13. If we were well accustomed to the exercise of the presence of God, all bodily diseases would be much alleviated thereby…. Take courage; offer Him your pains incessantly; pray to Him for strength to endure them. Above all, get a habit of entertaining yourself often with God, and forget Him the least you can. Adore Him in your infirmities…and in the height of your sufferings beseech Him humbly and affectionately (as a child his father) to make you conformable to His holy will. (12th Letter)

14. Ask of God, not deliverance from your pains, but strength to bear resolutely, out of love of Him, all that He should please, and as long as He shall please. (13th Letter)

15. Love sweetens pains; and when one loves God, one suffers for His sake with joy and courage. (13th Letter)

16. I have been often near dying, but I was never so much satisfied as then. Accordingly I did not pray for any relief, but I prayed for strength to suffer with courage, humility and love. Ah, how sweet it is to suffer with God! (14th Letter).

17. God knows best what is needful for us, and all He does is for our good. If we knew how much He loves us, we should always be ready to receive equally and with indifference from His hand the sweet and the bitter. (15th Letter).

John Bunyan (1628-1688) The Holy War

1. Satan's strategy to overthrow Mansoul once Emmanuel had rescued it: "Yea may we not by this means (by making wealthy) so bother Mansoul with abundance that they shall be forced to make their castle (place of prayer warfare) a warehouse instead of a

garrison fortified against us and a place where men of war stay....This advice was highly applauded by all (demons) and was accounted the very masterpiece of hell; namely to choke Mansoul with a fullness of this world and to fill her heart with the good things thereof." (Chap 16-p 298)

Duncan Campbell (1898-1971) – His Biography by Andrew Woolsley

1. It was Easter Monday 1952, and Duncan had just given an address at the Faith Mission Convention in Bangor, when he was suddenly arrested by a conviction that he should leave at once and go to Berneray, a small island off the coast of Harris with a population of about 400 people. "But Duncan, you can't go! You are booked to speak at the closing meeting!" Duncan responded, "I am sorry. I must go to Harris immediately... I must obey the promptings of the Spirit and go at once." He left the pulpit to pack his case and ...flew to Scotland. On Thursday morning he reached Harris and took the ferry to Berneray. He had never been there before and knew no one on the island.

2. The first person he met was a 16-year-old boy. "Could you direct me to the manse, please?" "The manse is vacant," the lad replied. "We have no minister just now. "The elders take the services. And one lives up the hill." Duncan asked, "Could you please go and tell him that Mr. Campbell has arrived on the island." Ten minutes later the boy came back to say that the elder was expecting him...and had arranged a service for 9:00 that night!

3. After a few uninspiring services, they were preparing to leave the church when the old man took off his hat, pointing to the direction the congregation had just left the service. "Mr. Campbell see what's happening! He has

come! He has come!" The Spirit of God had fallen upon the people as they moved down towards the main road and in a few minutes, they were so gripped with the subduing presence of God that no one could move any further.... Prayers ascended to God on the hillside. The entire island was shaken into a new awareness of God as many lives were saved and transformed during the following days. ... How glad Duncan was that he had responded to the Spirit's prompting. Had he remained to preach in Bangor he would never had reached Berneray in time to fulfill God's agreement with the elder. Obedience, even at the risk of misunderstanding, reaped its reward. (140-141).

4. The military flavor of Paul's epistles is inescapable. He draws uncompromising battle lines, pinpoints the tactics of the enemy, outlines the Christian's armor, and finally underlines the two essential weapons in aggressive spiritual warfare: the sword of the Spirit, which is the Word of God, and the artillery of prayer...To go to war without these is to court defeat. (151)

5. He never left the island without visiting the praying men, who had meant so much to him in the revival... He marveled at their discernment and world-wide vision in this far northwestern island. Calling to see one of them he arrived at the house to hear him in the barn praying for Greece. He could not understand what interest a butcher in Lewis could have in Greece. "How did you come to be praying for Greece today" he asked. "Do you know where Greece is?" "No, Mr. Campbell, but God knows, and He told me this morning to pray for Greece!"

6. Two years later Duncan was introduced to a man in Dublin who ... had gone to Greece on a business trip and was asked to speak to an assembly of Christians. The Spirit of God worked so powerfully that he continued preaching

for a few weeks.... Duncan compared the dates and discovered that the movement in Greece began on the same day that the butcher was praying in Barvas!" (161-162)

Timothy Dailey – Healing through the Power of Prayer

1. A Time/CNN poll of 1004 Americans revealed that 82%of the respondents believed in the healing power of prayer. In addition, 62%thought that doctors should be willing to pray for their patients. (10-11)

2. Dr James Krahn became interested in the subject after reviewing scientific studies showing that patients who are prayed for recover more clearly than those who are not. (12-13)

3. The majority of initial heart attacks occur on a Monday and are clustered between 8 and 9 AM...A Massachusetts study found that these Monday morning heart attacks were actually related to two key psychological factors: job dissatisfaction and lack of joy. (16)

4. As David B Larson says, I was told by my medical school professors that religion is harmful. Then I looked at the research, and religion is actually highly beneficial. If you go to church and pray regularly, it's very beneficial in terms of preventing illness, mental and physical, and you cope with illness much more effectively. (22)

5. 30 of the 126 medical schools in the country now have courses in faith and medicine. This seismic change is the result of a growing body of evidence confirming the healing power of prayer. (22)

6. Doctors use the term "spontaneous remission" when there is no known explanation for the disappearance of a known pathology. (45)

7. There are 41 distinct references to people being healed of various diseases in the gospels. A full 1/3 of the Gospel of Luke is devoted to Jesus' healings. (62)

8. In the OT alone there are more than 50 references to disease or pestilence being the result or threatened result of sin. (112)

9. Jesus came to bring the kingdom of God to earth. But before that could be accomplished, the kingdom of Satan had to be overturned. Jesus' earthly ministry constituted an assault upon the spiritual strongholds of evil. (121)

10. Don't give up if your prayers for healing aren't answered on the first attempt! (136)

11. Other alternatives to complete healing: First, is that the healing may take more time and prayer. (140)

12. Second, instead of total physical restoration, the healing may take the form of preventing further deterioration. (141)

13. Third we may be granted a temporary reprieve that can add productive years to our lives. (142)

14. There is one final possibility that most of us would prefer not to consider. ...That is, the healing that we receive may not be for our physical bodies but for our souls, to prepare us to meet our Maker peacefully and with a good conscience. (143)

15. If God heals us, it will be because of his sovereign will, not because we succeeded in striking a bargain with him. (157)

16. Make this oil a remedy for all who are anointed with it; heal them in body, in soul, and in spirit, and deliver them from every affliction. (175)

17. Just as we can have wrong motives in what we ask for, there can also be wrong motives in what we refuse to ask for. We can choose to remain sick and not to seek healing. (216)

18. Sickness can remain our subconscious safety valve to relieve us of unwanted responsibilities. (217)

19. No amount of prayer for physical or inner healing will be able to alleviate all our emptiness and struggle; the Cross is a reality in every Christian's journey. (229)

The Didache (ca 100 AD)

1. Do not keep the same fast days as the hypocrites. Mondays and Thursdays are their days for fasting, so yours should be Wednesdays and Fridays. (2:8)

2. Your prayers should be different from theirs. Pray as the Lord enjoined in His Gospel, thus: "Our Father, who art in heaven… Say this prayer three times a day. (2:8)

Mike Flynn – Making Disciples – 1997

1. As I have worked to be a disciple, and to make disciples, I have observed that Jesus practiced 7 behaviors as He made His disciples…. Only Jesus was perfectly competent in all seven of the methods by which He made disciples… Let me restate them: 1. I pray for them. 2. I recruit them. 3.

I hang out with them. 4. I teach them. 5. I apprentice them. 6. I debrief them. 7. I see that they get anointed. (8, 60-61)

Charles Hodge (1797-1878) – Princeton Sermons

1. Prayer – The prayerless Christian and the pulseless man are alike impossible. The pulse is the great criterion or index of the health of the body; so prayer is of the health of the soul. (293)

2. Priesthood of Believers – The OT priests were a distinct class, separated from the people. They could not engage in ordinary avocations, nor seek support in the ordinary way. Those who ministered at the altar were partakers of the altar. In like manner, Christians are a people separated from the world, and consecrated to God. They cannot belong to the world, seek its objects, or enjoy its pleasures. (193)

3. Walking with God – Walking with anyone is a familiar Scripture phrase for fellowship or communion. Walking with God, therefore, is habitual communion with him. (154)

4. Warfare (Spiritual) – If Satan is really the prince of the powers of darkness…; if he is the author of physical and moral evil; the great enemy of God, of Christ and of his people, full of cunning and malice; if he is constantly seeking whom he may destroy, seducing men into sin, blinding their minds and suggesting evil and skeptical thoughts; if all this be true, then to be ignorant of it, or to deny it, or to enter on this conflict as though it were merely a struggle between the good and the bad principles in our own hearts, is to rush blindfold to destruction. (376-377)

5. Warfare – Victory or Defeat? – The issue of the conflict is not uncertain. Christ has bruised Satan under our feet. If we resist in the strength of the Lord and in the use of his armor, we shall conquer. If we do not resist, or if the resistance is in our own strength or our own weapons, we shall perish. (91)

Frank Laubach (1937) – Letters by a Modern Mystic by son Robert Laubach

1. I like God's presence so much that when for a half hour or so He slips out of mind—as He does many times a day—I feel as though I have deserted Him, and as though I had lost something very precious in my life. (May 14, 1930)

2. I know that God is love-hungry, for He is constantly pointing me to some dull, dead soul which He has never reached and wistfully urges me to help Him reach… All day I see souls dead to God look sadly out of hungry eyes. (May 24, 1930)

3. I no longer feel in a hurry about anything. Everything goes right… Nothing can go wrong except one thing—that God may slip from my mind if I do not keep on my guard… My task is simple and clear. (May 24, 1930)

4. I must talk about God, or I cannot keep Him in my mind. I must give Him away in order to have Him. (June 1, 1930)

5. I have found such a way of life… And it is very simple, so simple that even a child could practice it. JUST TO PRAY INWARDLY FOR EVERYBODY ONE MEETS, and to keep on all day without stopping, even when doing other work of every kind. (Sept 28, 1931)

6. When I forget other people, I become fatigued rather quickly. When I am reminded of my purpose and start again holding people, seen and unseen, before God, a new exhilaration comes to me, and all the fatigue vanishes. (Sept 28, 1931)

7. Knowing God better and better is an achievement of friendship… How is it to be achieved? Precisely as any friendship is achieved—by doing things together. The depth and intensity of the friendship will depend upon variety and extent of the things we do and enjoy together. (Oct 11, 1931)

8. So if anybody were to ask me how to find God I should say at once, hunt out the deepest need you can find and forget all about your own comfort while you try to meet that need. Talk to God about it, and—He will be there. You will know it. (Oct 11, 1931)

9. But the most wonderful discovery of all is, to use the words of St Paul, "Christ lives in me." He dwells in us, walks in our minds, reaches out through our hands, speaks with our voices, IF we obey His every whisper. (102)

10. Christ is interested in every trifle, because He loves us more intimately than a mother loves her babe, or a lover her sweetheart, and is happy only when we share every question with Him. (103)

Andrew Murray (1828-1917) – The Authorized Biography by Leona Choy

1. The actual beginnings (of revival) were very quiet without any of the special means thought necessary to kindle the flame of spiritual life. Most of the congregations represented at the conference were those in which the awakening of religious fervor appears the earliest. This was seen initially in increased

attendance at prayer meetings, with many new prayer circles established. The congregations of Montagu and Worcester were first touched. (99)

2. But when God began to move in 1860, young and old, parents and children, without distinction of color, flocked to that prayer meeting, driven by a common impulse to cast themselves before God and utter their cries of repentance. (99)

3. In places where prayer meetings were unknown a year before, the people now complained because meetings ended an hour too soon! Not only weekly but daily prayer meetings were demanded by the people, even three times a day—and even among children. (99)

4. On a certain Sunday ... a colored girl of about 15 years of age, in service with a nearby farmer, rose at the back of the hall and asked if she too might propose a hymn. At first, I hesitated, not knowing what the meeting would think, but better thoughts prevailed, and I replied, Yes. She gave out her hymn verse and prayed in moving tones. While she was praying, we heard, as it were, a sound in the distance which came nearer and nearer, until the hall seemed to be shaken; with one or two exceptions, the whole meeting began to pray, the majority in audible voice, but some in whispers. Nevertheless, the noise made by the concourse was deafening. A feeling which I cannot describe took possession of me. Even now 43 years after these occurrences, the events of the never-to-be-forgotten night pass before my mind's eye like a soul-stirring panorama. I feel again as I felt then, and I cannot refrain from pushing my chair backwards, and thanking the Lord fervently for His mighty deeds. (Rev JC deVries of Worcester).

5. Prayer meetings were held every evening after that. It seems the pattern was the same each time, although no one set it. At the beginning of the meeting there was generally silence; no one made efforts to stir up emotions; but after the second or third prayer the whole hall would be moved as before, with no human prompting. Everyone would begin to pray aloud. (101-102)

Olea Nel – South Africa's Forgotten Revival (1860-61)

1. The article ended with the following call to prayer: "We earnestly beseech you to faithfully and fervently pray one hour every week, with others or alone, that God by His grace may visit our land and give us the blessing of the outpouring of the Holy Spirit just as He is presently doing in other parts of the world. (73)

2. One of the prerequisites of revival has always been prayer ... the Cape revival began in Montagu and Worcester where people had gathered for corporate prayer though they numbered but three or four. This is also exactly what happened in America... In Calvinia an inexplicable urge suddenly developed to form prayer meetings. This urge was particularly remarkable for this parish, as it had never shown any inclination to meet for prayer during the years that Hofmeyr had been its pastor. (84-85)

3. As the presence of God's Spirit started to grow in power, the prayer meetings multiplied and met up to three times daily. As one noted, "It was a time when many truly longed for salvation. A time when youth shared abundantly in God's blessing and many heathens were saved.... Early each morning and evening, people would make their way to prayer meetings. Children and young people would come

together pleading for mercy. Their hearts were warmed and charitable towards missions, and each sought the redemption of his unsaved brother. (91)

4. A year ago prayer meetings were unknown. Now they are held daily and sometimes as many as three times a day—even amongst children. (92)

Rosalind Rinker – Prayer – Conversing with God (1959)

1. Prayer is the expression of the human heart in conversation with God. The more natural the prayer, the more real He becomes. It has all been simplified for me to this extent: prayer is a dialogue between two persons who love each other. (23)

Rosalind Rinker – Communicating Love thru Prayer (1966)

1. When you pray, do you say what your heart wants to say? Or, ignoring your heart, do you pray for the ears of people? (16)

2. We could all listen to God speaking if we really wanted to. What miracles could take place if only we would listen! Learning to listen is part of learning to pray. (45)

3. Your mental attitude is half the battle. And you can learn to control your own conscious thoughts. (49)

4. Children have no self-consciousness. Adults are plagued with it. This is one of the reasons adults find communication difficult. Oh, to be a little child in God's presence. (60)

5. If prayer is talking to Jesus, why not stop praying and just talk to Him? (62)

6. We lack the simplicity to follow our hearts into the presence of Jesus who is always ready to make known His love for us. (63)

7. Listen to children pray and you'll know Jesus is real to them. They tell Him everything and no subject is considered out-of-bounds until they begin to imitate the prayers of their elders. Then, too often they begin to lose interest in church and religion altogether. (66)

Arthur Wallis – God's Chosen Fast

1. We have already noted that normally fasting is undertaken occasionally, as the need arises, and that it is a personal matter between the individual and God. The regular and public fasts, of which Scripture gives a number of examples, are obvious exceptions. (33)

2. If there is a local church threatened with discord and division, if spiritual life is waning and worldliness abounding, if conversions are few and backslidings frequent, would not this be a time when leaders should call that church to prayer and fasting? (37)

3. Fasting must be done unto God, even before the eye of the Father who sees in secret (Zech 7:5; Lk 18:11-12). (40-41)

4. God's chosen fast, then, is that which He has appointed; that which is set apart for Him, to minister to Him, to honor and glorify Him; that which is designed to accomplish His sovereign will. (43)

Dallas Willard (1935-2013) – Hearing God (1999)

1. My strategy has been to take as a model the highest and best type of communication that I know of from human

affairs and then place this model in the even brighter light of the person and teaching of Jesus Christ. In this way it has been possible to arrive at an ideal picture of what an intimate relationship with God is meant to be and also come to a clear vision of the kind of life where hearing God is not an uncommon experience.(10)

2. Hearing God is but one dimension of a richly interactive relationship, and obtaining guidance is but one facet of hearing God. (10)

3. The watchword of the worthy servant (Lk 17:7-10) is not mere obedience but love, from which appropriate obedience naturally flows.... The attitudes of the unprofitable servant...severely limits spiritual growth, unlike the possibilities of a life of free hearted collaboration with Jesus and his friends in the kingdom of heaven. (12)

4. The paradox about hearing God's voice must, then, be resolved and removed... (with) three general problem areas that must be briefly addressed: 1. What we know about guidance and the divine-human encounter from the Bible and the lives of those who have gone before us shows that God's communications come to us in many forms....2. we may have the wrong motives for seeking to hear from God....3. our understanding of God's communication with us is blocked when we misconceive the very nature of our heavenly Father and of his intent for us as his redeemed children and friends. (26-28)

5. Obviously, God must guide us in a way that will develop spontaneity in us. The development of character rather than the direction in this, that, and the other matter, must be the primary purpose of the Father. (E Stanley Jones, 28)

6. But if we allow God's conversational walk with us … to make us think that we are people of great importance, his guidance will pretty certainly be withdrawn. (38)

7. But now loneliness is loose on the landscape…. It is, as Mother Teresa of Calcutta once said, the leprosy of the modern world. (45)

8. Yet God's working through the Holy Spirit and the indwelling Christ to speak to us is not to keep us constantly under his dictation. Too much intrusion on a seed that has been planted, as on the life of a plant or child, simply makes normal, healthy growth impossible. (57)

9. A redemptive community consists not of robots but of mature people, who know how to live together and who know how to live with God. For that reason I think the model of a message a minute is mistaken and very harmful in our efforts to hear God. (58)

10. Our reverence for and faith in the Bible must not be allowed to blind us to the need for personal divine instruction within the principles of the Bible yet beyond the details of what it explicitly says. (59)

11. There are now more than 2500 distinct cults active in the United States alone, most based on the premise that God speaks to one or several central people in the group in a way that he does not speak to the ordinary members. (82)

12. But a major point of this book is that the still, small voice—or the interior or inner voice, as it is also called— is the preferred and most valuable form of individualized communication for God's purposes. (89)

13. We now turn to six ways in which people are addressed by God within the biblical record: (1) a phenomenon plus a voice, (2) a supernatural messenger or angel, (3) dreams

and visions, (4) an audible voice, (5) the human voice, (6) the human spirit or the "still small voice." (91)

14. Chapter 8 will deal at length with the question of how we can know which thoughts are from God.... Although reoccurring thoughts are not always an indication that God is speaking, they are not to be lightly disregarded. (102)

15. God is not impassive toward us like an unresponsive pagan idol; he calls us to grow into a life of personal interchange with him that does justice to the idea of our being his children. (105)

16. As Bible history proceeds, we notice that in the process of divine communication the greater the maturity of the listener, the greater the clarity of the message and the lesser the role played by dreams, visions and other strange phenomena and altered states. (110)

17. Once we are earnestly seeking God and get beyond the need to have big things happening to reassure us that somehow we are all right—and possibly that others are not—then we begin to understand and rejoice that, as Jesus so clearly lived and taught, the life of the kingdom is "righteousness, peace and joy in the Holy Spirit" (Rom 14:17) (114-115)

18. God created, God rules and God redeems through his word. (118)

19. I believe this (Mk 9) is an illustration of the principle that there are degrees of power in speaking the word of God and that prayer is necessary to heighten that power. Prayer is more fundamental in the spiritual life than is speaking a word and indeed is the indispensable foundation for doing so. (134)

20. Until now we have been dealing with the word of God as it comes to, upon and through us. But in the progress of God's redemptive work communication advances into communion and communion into union. When the progression is complete, we can truly say, "It is no longer I who live, but it is Christ who lives in me" (Gal 2:20) and "For me, living is Christ" (Phil 1:21.) (155)

21. Many discussions about hearing God's voice speak of 3 points of reference, also called "three lights" that we can consult in determining what God wants us to do. These are circumstances, impressions of the Spirit and passages from the Bible. When these 3 points in the same direction, it is suggested that we be sure the direction they point is the one God intends for us. (170)

22. I am led to the following conclusion: Direction will always be made available to the mature disciple if without it serious harm would befall people concerned in the matter or the cause of Christ. (200-201)

Appendix Six
Praying through the Kingdom Parables

20 Parables of the Kingdom*

Matthew

13:1-11, 18-23 (Parable of the Sower)

13:24-30 (Parable of the Weeds-explained 13:36-43)

13:31-32 (Parable of the Mustard Seed); Mk 4:30-32; Lk 13:18-19

13:33 (Parable of the Yeast); Lk 13:20-21

13:44 (Parable of the Hidden Treasure)

13:45-46 (Parable of the Pearl of Greatest Value)

13:47-50 (Parable of the Net)

18:1-6, 12-14 (Parable of the Wandering Sheep)

18:21-35 (Parable of the Unmerciful Servant)

20:1-16 (Parable of the Workers in the Vineyard)

21:28-32 (Parable of the Two Sons)

21:33-44 (Parable of the Tenants); Mk 12:1-11; Lk 20:9-18

22:1-14 (Parable of the Wedding Banquet)

25:1-13 (Parable of the 10 Virgins)

25:14-30 (Parable of the Talents); Lk 19:12-27

Mark

4:26-29 (Parable of the Growing Seed)

Luke

14:15-24 (Parable of the Great Banquet)

15:1-7 (Parable of the Lost Sheep)

15:8-10 (Parable of the Lost Coin)

15:11-32 (Parable of the Lost/Prodigal Son)

*When disciples asked Jesus how they should pray, He gave them **The Lord's Prayer.** In it, Jesus commanded us to pray, "Your kingdom come." (Luke 11:2). Long time global disciple makers, David and Paul Watson, write, "Jesus prayed, *Your kingdom come, your will be done on earth as it is in heaven (Matt 6:10).* Using the parables of the Kingdom of heaven (God) as prayer guides is an effective way to pray for your neighborhood [country, world]." (Contagious Disciple Making, p 86).

So, we often begin DMM Prayer times reading one of the Parables of the Kingdom because they reveal what the Kingdom of God or Heaven looks like. What we want on earth is just that, for God's Kingdom to come. After reading the parable, we spend a bit of time praying through the parts of the parable that strike us as being relevant to the Kingdom advancement we are seeking in our families, neighborhood, region and world. This sometimes takes the form of praise and other times of petition or request. After a few minutes, say 5-10 minutes, of this Kingdom prayer, we move on to specific petitions or intercession for specific people, places and things, always mentioning the one great request of The Harvest Prayer: "Lord of the harvest, send us and other laborers out into the harvest today."

I used the list of *Parables of Jesus* (p. 1602) in the NIV Study Bible to help compile this list.

Endnotes

[1] A phrase used by Jerry Trousdale and others, Miraculous Movements, pp 9, 38, 179. Mission agencies and parachurch organizations like the following have in whole or in part adopted the planting and promoting of Disciple Making Movements (DMMs) as their strategy: All Nations, The Bonhoeffer Project, CDM (Contagious Disciple Making), Compassion for Life, CRU, D6 Family, Dandelion Resourcing, discipleFIRST, Discipleship.org, Discipleship for Women, Downline Ministries, Emotional Healthy Discipleship, Every Square Inch Ministries, Exponential, Faith International University, Final Command, Freedom in Christ, Frontiers, Global Catalytic Ministries, Global Discipleship Initiative, Global Frontier Missions, Great Commandment Network, Impact Discipleship Ministries, IDMI (International Disciple Making Initiative), International Project, Leadership Network, Legacy Discipleship, Life-on-Life Missional Discipleship, LifeWay, Like Jesus Initiative, Lionshare, Mission Frontiers, Multiplyvineyard.org, Navigators Church Ministries, Radical Mentoring, Relational Discipleship Network, Renew Network, Replicate, Small Circle, Sonlife, TCM International, Untangle Addictions, YWAM Frontier Missions. This very partial list is growing daily.

[2] See my "Disciples Obey" (Xulon Press, 2015)

[3] Jerry's book has been pivotal in my life and many others who have come to embrace the concepts of DMMs, DBS (Discovery Bible Studies), People of Peace, Healing Prayer and that every Christian should be a disciple who makes disciples. I cannot recommend it too highly. All of its stories of the miraculous have been corroborated by independent researchers.

[4] Miraculous Movements, pp 24-25

[5] Debby, I and other colleagues will host or come to your venue and, without financial demands, introduce you to the amazing ancient world of New Testament Discipleship and the present world of Disciple Making Movements.

[6] See my discussion of these 4 steps in *Are You a Christian or a Disciple?* chapter 15

[7] See "Prayer in the Life of Jesus," Appendix 5 in *Are You a Christian or a Disciple?*

[8] The seminarian's name was Ed Saadi and he shared 1 Thes. 3:12 with me as his prayer for me. The youth director, fresh from ministering in New York City in Tim Keller's church, was Ryan Tompkins. Neither of these men probably realize just how God used them in a faithful moment in my life. One discussion with Ed and one sermon from Ryan began to change everything. We never know how God can use one conversation!

[9] Experiencing and praying through Robert Lewis's video series "Men's Fraternity" with scores of other men—and sharing my growth with Debby—were used by God to set me free.

[10] "Let Love Win through YOU" Published and available through Lulu Press in 2010

[11] Some manuscript texts read "seventy others"

[12] Disciples expected to reproduce, that is, to make more disciples – see Matt 23:25; Acts 2:11; 6:5; 13:43; 20:30. Also note from the Mishnah - Aboth 1:1 – "Moses received the Law from Sinai and committed it to Joshua, and Joshua to the elders, and the elders to the Prophets; and the Prophets committed it to the men of the Great Synagogue. They said three things: Be deliberate in judgement, raise up many

disciples, and make a fence around the Law." (Mishnah – ca 200 AD).

[13] The difference between today's church-going Christians and Jesus' first disciples is the focus of "Are You a Christian or a Disciple?" Xulon Press, 2014. In it the definition of "disciple" as used in the New Testament is clearly shared, surprising the reader of how different a disciple may be from a Christian today.

[14] David Watson in "Contagious Disciple Making," Introduction, xi

[15] Contagious Disciple Making, xiii

[16] From Chapter one of Miraculous Movements, p 20

[17] Miraculous Movements, p 24

[18] Read *Miraculous Movements* for a further description of Discovery Bible Study (DBS) and why they can be used anywhere in the world by anyone, even illiterate disciples, who want to make disciples!

[19] Delmarva is the 3 state, eastern shores peninsula area bordered by the Chesapeake Bay and the Atlantic Ocean. It has 14 counties, the 3 counties of DE, 9 eastern shore counties of MD and 2 of VA, hence, Delmarva. The population of Delmarva is less than 1 million people. Our mission is "to follow Jesus and make disciples of love throughout Delmarva who will advance His Kingdom by multiplication and missional unity." If you are interested in becoming part of this disciple making mission, contact me at ed.gross@comcast.net

[20] See my "Fruitful or Unfruitful: Why it really Matters" (Parsons Porch Publishing, 2017)

[21] The Systematic Theology of Charles Hodge, abridged, p 41.

[22] Miraculous Movements, pp 30-31

[23] Miraculous Movements, p 58

[24] Miraculous Movements pp 26-31

[25] Miraculous Movements p30

[26] Contagious Disciple Making, p 79

[27] Contagious Christianity, p 79

[28] The Christian Post, March 15, 2020

[29] "Pygmies" are tribes averaging height is 4'11" or less. Being spread across 14 countries in Africa, most of the 984,000 Pygmies live in 6 Central African countries.

[30] The Christian Post, March 15, 2020

[31] See *The Kingdom Unleashed* by Trousdale, Sunshine and Benoit (2018)

[32] The Christian Post, March 15, 2020

[33] For further instruction on discipling through DBS (Discovery Bible Studies),the method of discipling used by many in DMMs, see Miraculous Movements by Jerry Trousdale or simply access "Discovery Bible Study" on the worldwide web.

[34] "The Cost of Discipleship" by Dietrich Bonhoeffer; All the books written by Bill Hull on discipleship, but especially his, "The Complete Book of Discipleship"; "Great Commission Disciple Making" by Jim Lilly; "Becoming a Disciple Maker" by Bobby Harrington; "Making Disciples" by Ralph Moore;" The Lost Art of Disciple Making" by Leroy Eims; "Making

Radical Disciples" by Daniel Lancaster; "Disciple Shift" by Putnam and Harrington; etc.

[35] "Praying in the Holy Spirit" is not a reference to "praying in tongues." But simply to prayer that is empowered and guided by the Holy Spirit in a disciple who is filled with the Holy Spirit.

[36] Why most Christians' Prayer are NOT Answered, 100 Days with Jesus, Appendix 9, p 450

[37] NIV Study Bible p 1536

[38] See "Groups of 12" by Joel Comiskey (1999) and "From 12 to 3" (2002)

[39] See my "The Amazing Love of Paul's Model Church" (Parsons Porch Book Publishing Co., 2017)

[40] The Power of One: Connecting with People of Peace. Acquire from CRM Empowering Leaders – www.crmleaders.org

[41] The PoP question is, "Would you like to discover for yourself what God is like and how God wants you to live?" If the person is immediately ready, the follow-up question is, "Who could you invite to discover God with you?" Millions are being discipled today who have shown receptivity to those two questions.

[42] There is no better book than Miraculous Movements, but there are many others

CPSIA information can be obtained
at www.ICGtesting.com
Printed in the USA
LVHW021205040820
662306LV00001BA/177